As someone who grew up in the church, was raised on the Bible, and was taught to read it from cover to cover, I struggled as a kid and as an adult to get through parts of the Bible that made no sense or didn't seem relevant to me. How I wish a book like Alex Goodwin's *The Bible Reset* had come along. Whether you love reading the Bible or wish you did, *The Bible Reset* will forever change how you read the Bible. You'll be drawn into the grand story God is telling that centers on Jesus. You may even get a bit of help from Hobbits.

CAROLYN CUSTIS JAMES, author of *Half the Church* and *Malestrom*

The people of God have long affirmed how crucial the Bible is to understanding and living our faith. We often hear that the Bible is a remarkable gift. But honestly, it can be a strange book—ancient and sometimes hard to understand. The research is clear that people don't read it very much. Even those who try will too often struggle because they've been taught shortcuts that are untrue to what the Bible is. Alex Goodwin has set out to change this. He tells us the truth about the Bible: what it actually is and what we're supposed to do with it. He writes with clarity, grace, and humor. This book is fun and insightful, bold and necessary. If the Bible is going to make a comeback, Goodwin shows us how.

GLENN PAAUW, senior fellow at the Institute for Bible Reading

With an honest, accessible, and instructive approach, *The Bible Reset* explains that while our access to the Bible has never been easier, our understanding of *how* to engage with the Bible has

never been lower. If you feel guilty, frustrated, and dissatisfied with your level of engagement of Scripture, know that Alex offers weary Bible readers a hopeful way forward. Dig into this good book, and you'll learn to shift your perspective in order to dig deeper and engage further with the Good Book.

J.R. BRIGGS, founder of Kairos Partnerships and author of *The Sacred Overlap* and *Fail*

Alex Goodwin

Simple Breakthroughs
to Make Scripture
Come Alive

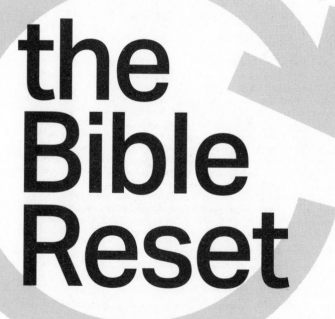

the
Bible
Reset

NavPress

A NavPress resource published in alliance
with Tyndale House Publishers

NavPress.com

The Team:
David Zimmerman, Publisher; Deborah Sáenz Gonzalez, Acquisitions Editor; John Greco, Copyeditor; Olivia Eldredge, Operations Manager; Lindsey Bergsma, Designer; Sarah K. Johnson, Proofreading Coordinator

Cover design by Lindsey Bergsma

Author photo copyright © 2021 by Cherie Miracle. All rights reserved.

Published in association with the Institute for Bible Reading

Some of the anecdotal illustrations in this book are true to life and are included with the permission of the persons involved. All other illustrations are composites of real situations, and any resemblance to people living or dead is purely coincidental.

For information about special discounts for bulk purchases, please contact Tyndale House Publishers at csresponse@tyndale.com, or call 1-855-277-9400.

ISBN 978-1-64158-736-5

Printed in the United States of America

29	28	27	26	25	24	23
7	6	5	4	3	2	1

For Lacey—
forever my first reader,
relentless encourager,
best friend.

Contents

PART ONE

form

We Can Do Better

What he greatly thought, he nobly dared.
HOMER

IT WAS A WEEK BEFORE CHRISTMAS 2016, and one of the wealthiest people in the world was stuck in traffic. Trapped on a Los Angeles highway, crawling behind the same car an inch at a time, he glared at the asphalt and tapped impatiently on his steering wheel. A world-renowned entrepreneur, he was accustomed to limitlessness. He had revolutionized entire industries, yet on this December morning he was reduced to helpless brooding in his car.

This is the twenty-first century, he must have thought, *in one of the richest, most powerful cities in the world. This*—this—*is the best we can do?* In that moment, he resolved to create a company to begin solving the problem of "soul-destroying traffic."[1]

Most of us can resonate with this feeling of frustration at something that was designed to help us but instead, at times, leaves us exasperated. The Bible is supposed to be our guide, yet we pick it up and, often, can't make it past a few paragraphs without getting distracted, bored, or confused. *Really—this is the best God could do?*

While you may not go so far as to call the Bible soul-destroying, you wouldn't be alone if your experience with this hyped-up book has been full of unmet expectations. Millions of people silently struggle with the Bible as they try their best to cultivate spiritual growth from this difficult text.

For all the glowing accolades Christians like to heap on the Bible—God-breathed, living and active, a lamp unto our feet—the actual task of reading it is really quite hard. It's not an easy book to begin with: It's an enormous book, full of smaller books with their own seemingly disjointed agendas, composed and compiled thousands of years ago and half a world away. If we manage to read it for any length of time, we encounter an abundance of strange stuff, boring stuff, and unsettling stuff. If we're honest, our thoughts can range from perturbed (*Oh great, the Philistines are attacking* again) to disturbed (*Wait, God did* what *to those people?*).

Nowadays, there are a few common reactions to the Bible's seemingly insurmountable challenges. One of them is to dismiss the Bible altogether. Over the last generation or two, the Good Book has been recast as the Obsolete Book, or even the Harmful Book. Some people are inclined to think, *It supports slavery. It's misogynistic. It's anti-science. Maybe it had a place in antiquity, but we've advanced beyond that now.* My generation, the millennials, is leading the charge away from the Bible and out of the church. *We'll find our sense of meaning somewhere else, thank you very much.*

Another reaction is shame. Nobody seems to be talking about how hard the Bible is, so we assume the problem must be with *us*.

Maybe we're not smart enough or disciplined enough or spiritual enough to really stick with it, to buckle down and come to appreciate this book.

So we make do. In the churning ocean of our strange and difficult Bible, we cling to a life raft of carefully curated greatest hits: John 3:16; Jeremiah 29:11; Philippians 4:13; a few psalms; maybe some of our favorite stories. Or we simply step back and leave the Bible to the experts, dining exclusively on the pre-chewed version explained by our pastor or YouTube videos or devotional books.

Confused. Angry. Apathetic. If any of this sounds familiar, I think this book can help. Because here's the secret: You've been set up for failure.

From the moment you open the Bible, the odds are stacked against you. The struggle begins with the formatting, which can resemble an overcrowded textbook more than anything else. On every page, you're confronted by stark pillars of text, often surrounded by a scaffolding of even more text: cross-references, notes, callout boxes, and more. Chapter and verse numbers swarm around the small print. The sheer volume of information is immediately overwhelming and unwelcoming. The simple act of reading is exhausting on its own—a literary Ironman Triathlon.

Beyond the difficult format, another hindrance is that most Christians never actually learn what they're supposed to do with the Bible or how to approach the strange, boring, or unsettling passages they encounter. For some reason, it's just assumed that if we open this book and spend enough time in it, the magic will happen. Like Chia Pet instructions to "just add water," we're taught to "just add Bible" and our faith will grow. We'll come to know God through this book if we just try hard enough.

For the first two decades of my life, the Bible was like the moon: always present but mysteriously distant. I grew up in a loving Christian home and attended a charming little church in northern Virginia. Every Sunday, we'd sit in the U-shaped balcony, singing out of our red hymnals and looking down on the rows of little old ladies in the pews, their cotton-ball hairstyles glowing in the morning light of the stained glass windows.

Before each sermon, our pastor would hold his Bible in the air and, with a good-natured grin and Southern twang, ask us to do the same: "Repeat after me. I believe the Bible. It is the Word of God. Where the Bible differs from my beliefs or my behaviors, *I can change*, through the power of the Holy Spirit."

I remember mornings spent in Sunday school, sitting in those tiny plastic chairs made for short legs and little butts while Miss Sandra and Miss Janet held up watercolor pictures and told us the story of Noah's Ark (well, the kid's version, at least). I remember countless Bible studies throughout high school and college, assembled in loose circles of futons and kitchen chairs, creeping chapter by chapter through some book of the Bible. Mostly, I remember the long, drawn-out silences after the study leader posed a question. We'd all stare at our feet or into our Bibles, feigning contemplation, hoping someone else would pipe up with a thought or an answer.

During all those years of sermons, Sunday school lessons, church programs, and Bible studies, I don't remember anyone ever explaining to me what the Bible actually *is*. Or addressing how unpleasant it was to read. Or helping me wrestle with all its weird and difficult stuff. And just to be clear, this isn't meant to be a criticism of my church or family or other ministries I've participated in. I'm telling you this because I think my experience is typical of the way things are. In many areas of Christian discipleship, the Bible is simultaneously the primary focus and the biggest blind spot.

Playing Bible Frisbee

In 2013, I gave my first honest assessment of this book that is God's Word. I'd finished college roughly a year earlier and immediately felt a pull to escape the stifling suburbs of my hometown. The pine trees, sunny skies, and crisp mountain air of Colorado were practically screaming my name.

In my zeal for new beginnings, I packed a couple of suitcases and flew across the country without a car, house, or job lined up—and without much of a plan for how I would acquire any of them. Thankfully, God provided the car and the home without much hassle. But he prescribed a long season of waiting for the job.

After nearly six months in Colorado, I had no real job prospects. I had graduated with honors from a good business school, but that apparently wasn't enough to warrant even a phone interview for a mind-numbing, entry-level position. I was halfway across the country, thousands of miles from my family and friends, trying my best to get started on a new life but getting nowhere. Maybe this had all been a big mistake.

I needed to hear from God—a word of reassurance, encouragement, truth, guidance, *something*. So I did the only thing I could think to do. Sitting quietly on the edge of my bed, I placed my brown, leather-bound Bible on my lap and took a deep breath. With one hand gripping the spine, I closed my eyes and bent the cover back, pressing my thumb into the edge of the pages and feeling them zip out from underneath. I stopped about three-fourths of the way through. With my eyes still closed, I extended my index finger and placed it on a random spot on the page.

I opened my eyes and read the verse under my finger. "On the following day Paul went in with us to James, and all the elders were present."[2] I read it again, in case I'd somehow missed the spiritual epiphany. I read the rest of the chapter in case I'd been off by a few verses. Nothing. I slammed the book shut and tossed it across my room like a Frisbee, where it landed in a heap underneath a chair. "This thing is useless."

Eventually I picked up my Bible again, and although I had to acknowledge the flimsiness of my point-and-pray technique, my larger questions remained. If the Bible is so important, why is it such a struggle to read? Why do I so often end up confused, frustrated, and bored?

A few weeks later, one of my friends handed me a Bible that looked different and read differently than any Bible I'd ever seen. There were no numbers anywhere, no notes, no features of any kind. Nothing but the Bible text. "You've got a marketing degree, right?" she said. "Figure out how to get this into as many hands as possible." I started reading it and became engrossed. The stories flowed together like they never had before. I actually lost track of time reading the Bible.

Then she introduced me to Glenn Paauw, the guy who had created and published this strange edition of the Scriptures. Turns out he worked for a Bible publisher in town, where he'd been researching and experimenting with Bible engagement for over twenty years, and this new Bible was one of the results of his work. He was looking to fill a position in a new Bible-engagement department, and he ended up hiring me.

During my second day at my new job, Glenn came into my office (well, my cube) with a stack of a dozen books under his arm. "Anytime you're not working on a project," he said, "I want you to make your way through these books. Come talk to me whenever you have any questions." He left the stack on my desk, and I cocked my head to scan the titles: *The Drama of Scripture, The Bible Made Impossible, The Lost World of Scripture, After Chapters and Verses, The New Testament and the People of God, How to Read the Bible Book by Book,* and so on.

That day became a turning point. In the weeks and months of reading and conversation that followed, I discovered that the mental and practical framework I'd constructed for the Bible was, in fact, a shanty house. No wonder it was so difficult to read. No wonder I had such a hard time connecting with it. No wonder I was so frustrated! As I began to learn what the Bible actually is and what we're supposed to do with it, the words on its pages started lighting up those parts of myself that had previously lain dormant: curiosity and imagination.

In 2016, Paauw, a couple of other colleagues from the Bible-publishing industry, and I formed the Institute for Bible Reading, a nonprofit ministry dedicated to inviting people into God's transformative story by changing the way they read the Bible. We created a game-changing new Bible-reading platform called Immerse (which I'll tell you more about later).

I'm writing this book because I think my journey can also be your journey. It's a journey of recovering what we've lost, remembering what we've forgotten, and discovering what we never learned. It's a journey that will have us removing the barriers that make the Bible seem like a difficult and frustrating book. Along the way, we'll open the wardrobe doors to an enchanted world ripe for exploration and discovery.

This book is divided into three parts that build upon one another. First, we'll take a hard look at the physical form of our Bibles. Why does this ancient library of stories, songs, letters, and other types of literature look so much like a phone book? What does a reference-manual Bible tell us we're supposed to do with it? And what would happen if we reverse engineered the Bible into something that was actually readable?

Second, once we have a more readable Bible, we'll be able to recover lost Bible-engagement habits: reading whole books from beginning to end, reading and discussing Scripture in community, receiving the Bible's literature on its own terms, and understanding the basics of cultural context. Without needing to become Bible scholars (but with a commitment to ongoing learning), we'll develop some foundational habits and practices for reading well.

Finally, once we're equipped with the right tools and essential practices, we'll get acquainted with the Bible's lifeblood: its story. Yes, the Bible is full of truth, wisdom, encouragement, guidance, and correction. But all those vital elements are contained within the Bible's story, the V6 turbo engine roaring inside, giving the whole thing life and power. It's a roller-coaster saga, full of laboring progress and huge setbacks, pandemic brokenness and glimmers of light. Shining at the center of it all is Jesus, God's living Word and clearest revelation. He is the key to understanding and interpreting the entire story.

Perhaps most exciting, the Bible's story is not one we observe from a distance, hoping to pick out bits and pieces for personal application. Instead, we'll discover that it's an unfinished drama. God has given us an invitation to join him in his cosmic restoration project, and it can completely redefine our lives if we choose to accept it. We don't simply read the Bible to understand and learn; we read it to live.

My wife went to college at Loyola Marymount University in the heart of Los Angeles, just a few minutes away from the LAX airport. One day after I returned from a work trip to LA, I was ranting about how much time we had wasted sitting in traffic. I asked her, "How on earth did you put up with that for four years?" She shrugged. "You just learn to deal with it. You factor it in to your travel and figure out ways to pass the time. I usually called my mom."

Over the years, I've come to realize just how crummy of a hand the average Christian has been dealt with the Bible. Thankfully, we don't have to accept the status quo and "learn to deal with" the circumstances we've inherited. Unlike the billionaire referenced earlier, we don't need to build a tunnel-carving machine and innovate a Bibleless alternative. Instead, as C. S. Lewis wrote in *Mere Christianity*, "If you are on the wrong road, progress means doing an about-turn and walking back to the right road."[3]

The Bible can still speak to us today, and not in the minimalistic, cherry-picked ways we've been settling for. It can capture our hearts and captivate our minds. It can transform our communities by reorienting us around the epic story we've been adopted into. All this is possible. We just have to retrace our steps and find the right road.

Six Feet Under

The medium is the message.
MARSHALL MCLUHAN

IF YOU WERE TO WALK AROUND YOUR HOUSE and thumb through random books on bookshelves and tables, the odds are that all of them would be more readable than your Bible. With the possible exceptions of the *Encyclopaedia Britannica*, your college calculus textbook, and the repair manual for a 1996 Honda Civic, pretty much every published book is more readily positioned to be opened and enjoyed by your eyeballs than the average Bible.

As the written Word of the same God who created snowflakes and sunsets, blue jays and butterflies, why are the Scriptures so . . . ugly? Tiny print, two columns, thin paper, numbers large and small, section headings, footnotes, callouts, cross-references—not exactly begging to be read, is it?

Where did all this stuff come from? Paul certainly didn't write his letters to the Corinthians with chapter breaks and verse numbers. First Samuel didn't originally include spoiler-alert section headings like *Saul Tries to Kill David* or *David Spares Saul's Life* or *David Spares Saul Again*.

Yet this is the Bible we've inherited, and few of us have ever questioned it. We may even subconsciously assign a certain degree of authority to the Bible's fortress-like appearance. If the Bible is a stronghold of truth, a bastion of divine revelation, then of course it should look imposing.

But for scores of people, the Bible's format has made the possibility of actually reading the text a nonstarter. The fortress walls have not been an assurance of authority but a barricade that says Keep Out. We're told that Bible reading is a central practice of the Christian faith, yet the physical appearance of our Bibles actively works against our twin goals of reading and comprehension.

It wasn't always like this. A brief exploration into the Bible's history shows us that the real Bible has been buried for five hundred years, and we're holding the shovel. The very first step in our journey toward better Bible reading is diagnosing the deficiencies of our modern Bibles. Before we can equip ourselves with new tools, we need to understand why the old ones haven't been working.

A Flyby History of the Modern Bible

Truth be told, scribes have been subdividing the Bible since its inception. According to biblical scholar Christopher Smith, "The entire Old Testament except for Psalms was divided into paragraphs (or *parashoth*) even before the time of Christ."[1] The New Testament was split into topical sections called *kephalaia* around the fourth century.

These and other marking systems were added to help with the public reading of Scripture, giving the reader guidance on places to pause and breathe or end the day's reading. Most hearers weren't even aware that these markings existed, and they were certainly never considered an intrinsic part of the text.

Everything began to change around AD 1200, when Stephen Langton developed the modern Bible-chapter system. If your reaction is "Wow, that's actually pretty recent," you're not wrong.

Langton was an English church leader, a professor at the University of Paris, and a prolific Bible scholar. To help with his work writing Bible commentaries, Langton decided to split each book of the Bible into relatively uniform numbered chunks that he and others could use to easily reference specific passages. There had been other chapter arrangements before Langton's, but his system stuck, and his numbers are what appear in our modern Bibles today.

Chapters and verses may go together like burgers and fries, but verses are actually about three hundred years younger. Our modern verse system was developed in the mid-1500s by Robert Estienne, a French printer and classical scholar. Estienne was working on a Bible concordance, which is a reference tool primarily used for finding the instances where specific words appear in Scripture. If you need to know every place the word *grace* is used, for example, you can look it up in a concordance and find a list of the locations.

Langton's chapter system was a nice start, but Estienne needed even more precision. Langton introduced zip codes to the Bible, but Estienne needed street addresses. He needed a reference system that would allow users to immediately locate a hyper-specific portion of Scripture to find the exact word they were looking for. So, during a three-hundred-mile journey from Paris to Lyon, he began his project to add this new subset of verse numbers to the New Testament, working within Langton's chapters and marking off a new verse after every sentence or two. He finished in ten days.

Nearly forty years after Estienne's death, his son Henri praised the invention of verse numbers in the second edition of the concordance: "As that invention came to light it had everyone's appreciation and attained such authority that other editions of the New Testament . . . lost their significance if they did not follow this invention."[2]

He was right. Langton's chapter system and Estienne's verse system were paired together during a period of extreme innovation for the Bible. The printing press had been invented roughly a hundred years earlier, launching the Bible on a new trajectory of rapidly increasing availability and affordability. New translations were emerging in familiar languages like English, Italian, and German, rather than the traditional Latin. For the first time in history, the Bible was making its way into the hands of the common people in languages they could understand, and nearly every copy was printed with a chapter-and-verse reference system.

The ancient Scriptures had been recast, as Smith summarizes, "to reflect two key values of modernity: information and speed."[3]

In 1560, the Geneva Bible was printed in two columns (which allowed more words to fit on a page, thus saving on paper costs) with each verse indented as its own independent paragraph. If a verse break came in the middle of a sentence, the sentence was broken in half with a new line. What had once been the rolling narratives of the Gospels or thundering warnings of the Prophets were industrialized into uniform blocks of numbered statements, indistinguishable from book to book. As Joni Mitchell sang in "Big Yellow Taxi," "They paved paradise and put up a parking lot."[4]

The Bible as Technology

In his groundbreaking book, *The Shallows: What the Internet Is Doing to Our Brains*, Nicholas Carr spends some time exploring the relationship between humans and the technologies we create. "Every technology is an expression of human will," he says. "Through our tools, we seek to expand our power and control over our circumstances—over nature, over time and distance, over one another."[5]

He classifies technologies into four different categories. The first extends our physical capabilities: the plow, the crowbar, or the ladder, for example. The second extends the range or sensitivity of our five senses: the microscope, the telescope, the Geiger counter. The third set actually reshapes nature to better serve our needs or desires: birth control pills, dams, genetically modified foods.

For the fourth category, he borrows a term used by anthropologists and sociologists: *intellectual technologies*. These tools are used to extend or support our mental abilities—to work within the realms of information and ideas, to share knowledge and articulate belief. Think of the typewriter, the globe, and yes, the book.

While any tool can influence us on some level, it's these intellectual technologies that have the most deeply formative impact on who we are as people and societies. When new intellectual technologies, like the computer or the clock, are introduced to the world, everything changes. Not only in production and efficiency but in how our minds and cultures actually operate. "The tools we use to write, read, and otherwise manipulate information work on our minds even as our minds work with them."[6] In other words, over time we become more and more like our tools.

Every intellectual technology has an embedded *intellectual ethic*:

a set of assumptions about how the human mind works or should work. Inventors of intellectual technologies are usually so focused on solving immediate problems that they don't pause to consider the assumptions baked into their creation or the by-products that will result from their use. The people who use these tools normally aren't aware either; like the inventors, they are too excited about the practical benefits of their new device to worry much about its side effects.

For example, think about how the invention of the mechanical clock changed our relationship to time. Although there were ancient timekeeping instruments like obelisks, sundials, and water clocks, for the vast majority of people throughout history, the measurement of the passing of time was loosely governed by the movements of the sun, moon, and stars. Light and darkness. We were tied to the natural rhythms of the earth, and life was, as French medievalist Jacques Le Goff wrote, "dominated by agrarian rhythms, free of haste, careless of exactitude, unconcerned by productivity."[7] Today, the clock has exactified time into a measurable resource. Time is mechanical. Synchronized. As a result, humans have become highly efficient, precise, and productive creatures. Just like our clocks.

However, in our mastery of time, we have simultaneously enslaved ourselves to it. "How serenely the hands move with their filigree pointers, and how steadily!" writes Mary Oliver. "Twelve hours, and twelve hours, and begin again! Eat, speak, sleep, cross a street, wash a dish! The clock is still ticking."[8] We are beholden to our clocks, rising not when the sun comes up but because our alarm clocks tell us to. We don't eat lunch because we're necessarily hungry but because it's twelve o'clock. "The town's clock cries out, and the face on every wrist hums or shines; the world keeps pace with itself. Another day is passing, a regular and *ordinary* day."[9] Our mechanical clocks have turned us into creatures of precision and order, which has brought a number of benefits to society. But what have we lost?

All right, enough about clocks. What can this example illustrate about our modern Bible? What is its intellectual ethic? What did embedding a foreign reference system directly into the text assume about the character of the Scriptures? What does it signal to us about the way humans should engage with these inspired words? What by-products has it created? How has it impacted the ways we find truth and explore meaning? How has it changed the way we know God? We don't have the time or space to explore each of these questions here, but they're worth our sober reflection.

What Carr doesn't explore, and what doesn't apply to any of these other technologies, is the innovation of an artifact that already bears the fingerprints of the Divine. If we believe the Bible is inspired, then we must believe that God was involved not only in *what* the authors communicated but in *how* they communicated it. God's Word to us has never been mere information to be telepathically uploaded into our brains. He chose to communicate through literature, through the stories and letters and songs and prophecies of an ancient people. Does the modern Bible honor that choice?

We don't have to look far to see how chapter divisions fail to line up with the natural contours of the text. In fact, we can turn to page 2. The Bible's very first chapter break, at Genesis 2, comes four verses too early, before the opening week of Creation is actually finished. The famous Suffering Servant song in Isaiah 53 actually begins in Isaiah 52. Because chapters are designed to be the same length generally, throughout the Bible they incorrectly split up longer passages and combine shorter ones. Using them as reading guides is unreliable at best and misleading at worst.

Verses arguably do a more egregious job of chopping up the text than chapters since, again, they are a tool designed for uniformity and not necessarily congruence with the content itself. To borrow a small example from Christopher Smith:

> "The statements numbered 1 Corinthians 6:19-20 in the traditional system, if divided reasonably into two verses, would read something like this:
>
> (19) Do you not know that your bodies are temples of the Holy Spirit, who is in you, whom you have received from God?
>
> (20) You are not your own; you were bought at a price. Therefore honor God with your bodies.
>
> Unfortunately, the verse divisions were placed here instead:
>
> (19) Do you not know that your bodies are temples of the Holy Spirit, who is in you, whom you have received from God? You are not your own;
>
> (20) you were bought at a price. Therefore honor God with your bodies."[10]

This example may seem relatively inconsequential, but what happens when our brains must constantly accommodate for this odd and arbitrary system? How does it impact our experience when we're forced to navigate a text littered with speed bumps and stop signs? There are already challenges to reading and understanding this ancient literature; using chapters and verses as intentional units of the Bible that guide our reading only introduces extra hurdles and obstacles.

We could go down the list of modern additives—section headings, footnotes, cross-references, and so on—and show how their *intellectual ethics* influences the ways we engage with Scripture. Each of them can certainly be useful within the narrow purpose of their design, but all too often they end up either distracting us or obscuring the meaning of the text. Or both.

To illustrate, take a look at the side-by-side rendering of Charles Dickens's famous opening of *The Tale of Two Cities* on the following pages.[11] On the left, you will see Dickens's work in its natural format, and on the right you'll see it adapted into a standard Bible format. What's your visceral reaction? What signals do the left- and right-hand pages send about what you're supposed to do with the words on the page?

Isn't it curious that no other types of literature have adopted the modern Bible's "innovations" as ways to improve the reader's interactions with the page? That writers and poets throughout the centuries and across the continents have unanimously decided that pumping a text full of numbers and notes does not constitute a better experience for the reader?

Yet the modern Bible has become such a staple of modern Christianity that we're conditioned to accommodate its oddities and excuse its shortcomings. Many Christians are quick to say that they can ignore the reference numbers and footnotes, as if they were merely signs on the side of the highway. It's not until they're introduced to a different reading experience that they see how they've been battling obstacles the entire time.

It was the best of times,
it was the worst of times,
it was the age of wisdom,
it was the age of foolishness,
it was the epoch of belief,
it was the epoch of incredulity,
it was the season of Light,
it was the season of Darkness,
it was the spring of hope,
it was the winter of despair,
we had everything before us, we had nothing before us, we were all going direct to Heaven, we were all going direct the other way—in short, the period was so far like the present period, that some of its noisiest authorities insisted on its being received, for good or for evil, in the superlative degree of comparison only.

There were a king with a large jaw and a queen with a plain face, on the throne of England; there were a king with a large jaw and a queen with a fair face, on the throne of France. In both countries it was clearer than crystal to the lords of the State preserves of loaves and fishes, that things in general were settled for ever.

It was the year of Our Lord one thousand seven hundred and seventy-five. Spiritual revelations were conceded to England at that favoured period, as at this. Mrs. Southcott had recently attained her five-and-twentieth blessed birthday, of whom a prophetic private in the Life Guards had heralded the sublime appearance by announcing that arrangements were made for the swallowing up of London and Westminster. Even the Cock-lane ghost had been laid only a round dozen of years, after rapping out its messages, as the spirits of this very year last past (supernaturally deficient in originality) rapped out theirs. Mere messages in the earthly order of events had lately come to the English Crown and People, from a congress of British subjects in America: which, strange to relate, have proved more important to the human race than any communications yet received through any of the chickens of the Cock-lane brood.

The Paradox of our Times

1 *It was the best of times, it was the worst of times, ²it was the age of wisdom, it was the age of foolishness, ³it was the epoch of belief, it was the epoch of incredulity, ⁴it was the season of Light, it was the season of Darkness, ⁵it was the spring of hope, it was the winter of despair,* ⁶we had everything before us, we had nothing before us, ⁷we were all going direct to Heaven, we were all going direct the other way—in short, the period was so far like the present period, that some of its noisiest authorities insisted on its being received, ⁸for good or for evil, in the superlative degree of comparison only[a].

The Rulers of our Times

⁹There were a king with a large jaw and a queen with a plain face, on the throne of England[b]; ¹⁰there were a king with a large jaw and a queen with a fair face, on the throne of France[c]. ¹¹In both countries it was clearer than crystal to the lords of the State preserves of loaves and fishes, that things in general were settled for ever.

The Change of our Times

2 It was the year of Our Lord one thousand seven hundred and seventy-five. ²Spiritual revelations were conceded to England at that favoured period, as at this. Mrs. Southcott[d] had recently attained her five-and-twentieth blessed birthday, ³of whom a prophetic private in the Life Guards had heralded the sublime appearance by announcing that arrangements were made for the swallowing up of London and Westminster. ⁴Even the Cock-lane ghost had been laid only a round dozen of years, after rapping out its messages, as the spirits of this very year last past (supernaturally deficient in originality) rapped out theirs. ⁵Mere messages in the earthly order of events had lately come to the English Crown and People, from a congress of British subjects in America[e]: ⁶which, strange to relate, have proved more important to the human race than any communications yet received through any of the chickens of the Cock-lane brood.

⁷France, less favoured on the whole as to matters spiritual than her sister of the shield and trident, rolled with exceeding smoothness down hill, making paper money and spending it. ⁸Under the guidance of her Christian pastors, she entertained herself, besides, with such humane achievements as sentencing a youth to have his hands cut off, ⁹his tongue torn out with pincers, and his body burned alive, because he had not kneeled down in the rain to do honour to a dirty procession of monks which passed within his view, ¹⁰at a distance of some fifty or sixty yards. ¹¹It is likely enough that, rooted in the woods of France and Norway, there were growing trees, ¹²when that sufferer was put to death, already marked by the Woodman, Fate, to come down and be sawn into boards, to make a certain movable framework with a sack and a knife in it, terrible in history.

3 It is likely enough that in the rough outhouses of some tillers of the heavy lands adjacent to Paris, there were sheltered from the weather that very day, rude carts, bespattered with rustic mire, snuffed about by pigs, and roosted in by poultry, which the Farmer, Death, ²had already set apart to be his tumbrils of the Revolution. ³But that Woodman and that Farmer, though they work unceasingly, work silently, and no one heard them as they went about with muffled tread: ⁴the rather, forasmuch as to entertain any suspicion that they were awake, was to be atheistical and traitorous.

Lawlessness in England

⁵In England, there was scarcely an amount of order and protection to justify much national boasting. ⁶Daring burglaries by armed men, and highway robberies, took place in the capital itself every night; ⁷families were publicly cautioned not to go out of town without removing their furniture to upholsterers' warehouses for security; ⁸the highwayman in the dark was a City tradesman in the light, and, being recognised and challenged by his fellow- tradesman whom he stopped in his character of "the Captain," gallantly shot him through the head and rode away; ⁹the mall was waylaid by seven robbers, and the guard shot three dead, and then got shot dead himself by the other four, "in consequence of the failure of his ammunition:" ¹⁰after which the mall was robbed in peace; ⁷that magnificent

---

a. Here we see a description of a vision that human prosperity cannot be matched with human despair.

b. Referring to George the III, and his queen, Charlotte Sophia.

c. Referring to Louis XVI, and his consort, Marie-Antoinette.

d. An anachronistic reference as Joanna Southcott, who would not yet have been known as a prophetess in 1775, though readers in 1859 would have known her thus.

e. A list of "grievances" from British subjects in America, which preceded the Declaration of Independence the following year, 1776.

A Brief Digression

It wouldn't be fair to villainize the modern Bible as much as I have without a few concessions.

Using the description of intellectual technologies from earlier, it's fair to say that Langton's chapters and Estienne's verses were innocent enough in their own right. Their commentaries and concordances were specialized reference projects that needed corresponding reference systems, and the systems they created are quite good for their intended purpose: finding things quickly. The problems arose when somebody decided the specialized reference system needed to become a standard feature in every Bible and, eventually, be treated as a fundamental part of Scripture itself.

The modern Bible's reference tools have also played a valuable role in the development of the biblical scholarship we enjoy today. Giving scholars a system they can use to easily cite specific passages has allowed for collaboration and debate. These brilliant minds, then, build upon one another's work and help all of us better understand the Bible.

Finally, I should also note that some Bible publishers today have taken steps to address some of the modern Bible's issues. Many Bibles today are laid out in one column instead of two, allowing the reader's eyes to make it all the way across the page before having to drop down to a new line. Most Bibles place chapter numbers within the flow of the text rather than requiring a line break, and some attempt to make verse numbers less noticeable. But no matter how much we try to minimize their interruptions, our attempts to engage with the Bible are still governed by the artificial exoskeleton of chapters and verses.

The modern Bible has a role to play in the ecosystem of Scripture engagement. But for most of us, most of the time, it's simply incongruent with the goal of reading.

The Digitally Molded Mind

There's one more ingredient worth exploring in this cocktail of Bible confusion, which is this: Our attempts to read the Bible do not happen in a vacuum. We sit down and open these ancient texts in the midst of our everyday lives—lives increasingly governed by the universal presence of the internet.

Several centuries ago, Gutenberg's printing press launched a cultural revolution by rewiring people's brains to accommodate the neurological demands of books. In order to follow the flow of ideas presented over pages and pages of text, readers had to learn new methods of concentration, attentiveness, patience, and stillness. The Literary Mind was born.

William Shakespeare, Jane Austen, Charles Dickens, Mark Twain, Leo Tolstoy, Toni Morrison, Ernest Hemingway, Emily Dickinson, J. R. R. Tolkien, and many others crafted their masterpieces with the assumptions inherent to the Literary Mind. They trusted that readers engaging with their work would have the patience and concentration necessary to stick around as the stories unfolded. Until very recently, the Literary Mind reigned supreme.

Now the internet has become our cognitive home. In just a few short years, the Web has executed a neurological blitzkrieg, destroying our old mental pathways of focused attentiveness and rewiring us for the functions it demands. The concentration required by books has been replaced by the constant task switching and distractedness encouraged by the internet. Our quest for knowledge has moved from the slow, patient cultivation of a farmer to the frenetic chase of a hunter-gatherer. We zip from here to there, picking out information we find interesting or applicable and ignoring the rest.

A study by Time Inc. observed that people in their twenties switch media sources an average of twenty-seven times per hour and check their cell phones between 150 and 190 times per day.[12] Another study at the University of California, San Diego found that the average person consumes about thirty-four gigabytes (the equivalent of a hundred thousand words) of content per day.[13] The only way to attend to that volume of information is by training our brains to decrease the level of attention we devote to any of it.

Focused long-form reading is extremely difficult under these circumstances. Even if we're reading a paperback novel or a newspaper a hundred miles away from the nearest screen, the habits we've cultivated during our digital hours come with us. In the opening chapter of *The Shallows*, Carr admits his own experience: "Whether I'm online or not, my mind now expects to take in information the way the Net distributes it: in a swiftly moving stream of particles. Once I was a scuba diver in the sea of words. Now I zip along the surface like a guy on a Jet Ski."[14]

We have immediate access to more information than ever before, yet the surface-level engagement is not paying dividends. Studies show the kind of reading we're forced into online results in lower levels of comprehension and retention. Our brains have trouble storing information in long-term memory and forming the complex mental connections that constitute real knowledge. We are in a perpetual state of information overload, trying to process the myriad articles, hyperlinks, ads, images, browser tabs, text messages, emails, and other digital stimulation vying for our attention.

"Every medium has its strengths and weaknesses; every medium develops some cognitive skills at the expense of others," says UCLA psychologist Patricia Greenfield. "Although . . . the Internet may develop impressive visual intelligence, the cost seems to be deep processing: mindful knowledge, acquisition, inductive analysis, critical thinking, imagination, and reflection."[15]

Enter the modern Bible. In an era of distracted skimming, our Bibles could take a bold stand for concentration. They could, at every turn, fend off our minds' temptations to dart from stimulus to stimulus and invite us to focus on the inspired words of God. They could challenge us, amidst the clanging cacophony of Facebook and Instagram, to change our pace and lose ourselves in the epic tale of our Creator and his creation.

Instead, our Bibles roll over and surrender. In fact, it could be argued that the modern format of the Scriptures has been in the distraction business for centuries, long before the first *.com* was ever tapped on a keyboard. Our chapter-and-verse indexing system prioritized information, speed, and searching and finding long before Google did. The internet just supercharged it.

"Reading a regular Bible makes me tense," a high school sophomore once admitted to our team. "There's so much stuff on the page, and I don't really know what do to with it all. Do I read all the Bible text and then go back and read the footnotes? Do I stop and read the footnotes as I come across them? Do I need to look up the cross-references each time they're listed? Can I turn the page if I haven't read everything?"

This is a problem. We can do better.

Making Better Culture

In his book *Culture Making*, Andy Crouch reminds us that as image bearers of the Creator we also inhabit the world as creators. God gives us raw materials, and we are to use them to bring something into being that wasn't there before. God gives us eggs; *we* make omelets. God gives us trees; *we* make tables and chairs. God gives us steel; *we* make medical equipment. Or we make bullets and bombs. It's up to us. "Culture is what we make of the world."[16]

God inspired the words of Scripture, sometimes as stories told around a fire before being scratched onto stiff parchment and then read aloud in synagogue and sometimes as letters carried down dusty roads, then copied and distributed to churches around Asia Minor. Over time, these texts evolved into hand-copied books, then into printed books, and now into pixels on our smartphones.

The Bible isn't exempt from our creational domain. Have we done well with what we've made it into? Have our decisions about the physical appearance and features of our Bibles honored the true nature of its inspired words?

Folks like you and me find ourselves in an uphill battle that must be waged on two different fronts. The internet has made us forget how to read deeply, think clearly, and focus intently. And even if we try to go against the grain of our minds' distracted tendencies, even if we fight that inner resistance, our modern Bibles work against our goal of focused reading every step of the way.

For far too long, we've been ill-equipped for our task, hamstrung from our starting blocks. We've inherited a Bible that encourages distraction, hides the literature, and requires an inordinate amount of effort to sit and simply read.

Thankfully, as Christians, we are culture makers who believe in the power of resurrection. The Bible may be buried under centuries of additives, but we can recover what's been lost.

Digging Up the Real Bible

Critique by creating.
MICHELANGELO

IN 1512, MICHELANGELO FINISHED PAINTING the ceiling of the Sistine Chapel. Over the course of four years, he had adorned the massive vaulted surface with more than five thousand square feet of frescoes. Nine scenes from Genesis run down the middle, bordered by depictions of seven of Israel's prophets and five pagan sibyls said to have foretold the birth of Christ.

Near the center stretches *The Creation of Adam*, the most famous of the ceiling scenes. God, outstretched and aloft and clothed in only a simple tunic, reaches his strong right arm toward the naked Adam. The man, reclining on the ground, seems barely able to lift his own arm; his hand hangs lazily toward his Maker's. Their index fingers hover in space, not yet touching. The viewer is left to anticipate the explosive, electric contact that will be made between the giver of life and its recipient.

Michelangelo's ceiling is widely regarded as one of the finest artistic achievements in all human civilization—not bad for someone who considered himself more of a sculptor than a painter.

Of course, his masterpiece wasn't displayed in a modern, climate-controlled museum but rather in a functioning cathedral in the middle of a major city. Conditions were not ideal. Dust and soot built up from the candles burning below, water leaked through from the floor above, and cracks threatened the integrity of the plaster. When Michelangelo returned to the Sistine Chapel twenty years after he completed the ceiling, he was dismayed to find his work in such poor condition.

As the years passed, various popes approved efforts to preserve the artwork. Early conservators used chunks of bread dipped in wine to mop up the accumulated dirt and grit. They applied coats of linseed oil and varnish to counteract the grime that had built up from the water leaks. Perhaps the most disastrous measure was the use of a glue-like substance made of animal fat that was meant to mask water spots and brighten the colors but that inadvertently trapped dust and soot underneath. Over time, "the glue yellowed, hardened, and eventually cracked, becoming the nemesis of generations of restorers."[1]

The candles continued to burn. More recently, exhaust fumes from the modernizing city have made their way into the great cathedral. The frescoes became so uniformly dark that critics accused the great sculptor of having an insensitivity to color. With the average visitor only able to view the scenes from nearly seventy feet away on the cathedral floor, why would Michelangelo make everything so dark and dull? Nobody knew what the ceiling had once been.

A Different Kind of Bible

Our culture has a tendency to emphasize utility and practicality over beauty and structure. In her book *On Reading Well*, Karen Swallow Prior explains: "The content of a literary work is what it says; its form is how it is said. Unfortunately, we are conditioned today to focus on content at the expense of form."[2] As long as it works, who cares what it looks like? She continues:

> Reading virtuously requires us to pay attention to both
> form and content. And because literature is by definition
> an aesthetic experience, not merely an intellectual one, we
> have to attend to form at least as much as to content, if
> not more. Form matters.[3]

Form matters indeed. When it comes to the Bible, it's unfair and unrealistic to expect would-be readers to overcome the mental obstacle course of the modern Bible's design in order to engage deeply with its literature. In most cases, it's unnecessary to burden the sacred words with a pile of utilitarian "features" that overwhelm their natural beauty and structure. But for nearly half a millennium, we've struggled with the modern reference Bible because it's all we've had. We've become so used to the dark and drab ceiling frescoes that alternatives are rarely even considered.

The next step in our journey is to reclaim the Bible as a library of literature rather than simply an index of information. Before we move forward with anything else in this book, we need to equip ourselves with new intellectual technology. We need a reader's Bible.

Reader's Bibles are made to do exactly what the name suggests: provide the best reading experience possible. Instead of crowding the text with features that promote serial referencing, reader's Bibles give the ancient Scriptures room to breathe, proudly displaying the natural literature without any distractions.

Whether publishers recognize it or not, the process for creating a reader's Bible is governed by two guiding principles: *preservation of the sacred* and *elegant simplicity*.

To determine what is and isn't on the table for change, the first question that needs to be asked is *What is sacred and what is not?* Nothing can be added or taken away from the actual words of Scripture, of course, but what other changes can be made that will reveal rather than conceal the Bible's true nature?

Doing this work with integrity requires studying the Bible's history and its evolution as a book. None of the modern additives—chapters, verses, section headings, notes, cross-references, red letters, and so on—are sacred elements that need to be kept. But what about the order of books? What about book divisions? There are ways to innovate the Bible-reading experience that go beyond merely taking things out.

Elegant simplicity is the reason the little black dress will never go out of style. It represents neither frivolous adornment nor oversimplification but rather a critical eye for what's necessary. Steve Jobs championed elegant simplicity during his time at Apple, showcased in groundbreaking, user-friendly products like the Mac computer, iPod, and iPhone. In 1977, the headline to Apple's first marketing brochure proclaimed, "Simplicity is the ultimate sophistication."[4] Elegant simplicity is what good designers strive for—ruthlessly eliminating everything but the most essential components and displaying them in ways that make good sense instinctively.

The Bible is a big, complex book, but there are ways to recover a reading experience that is intuitive and natural, one that gives readers a way to interact with its elaborate content in a beautifully simple form.

The Beauty behind the Mask

When we formed the Institute for Bible Reading, our top priority was to create a best-in-class reader's Bible. In recent decades, a few editions of the Bible had been printed without chapter and verse numbers (the first copies of *The Message* translation were without chapter and verse at the insistence of Eugene Peterson), but most were viewed as novelty items. Some publishers elected to keep chapter numbers in the margins. We wanted to pull out all the stops.

As it turned out, getting rid of additives was pretty easy. Thanks to modern publishing software, we unchecked a few boxes in the settings menus and, one by one, the chapters, verses, headings, and other elements blinked out of existence. Eventually, we were left with nothing but the text. But we had a new problem.

Instead of the two stark pillars of cluttered, numbered text that adorn most modern Bibles, we now had a giant, single-column wall of words. Their faults notwithstanding, chapters, verses, and section headings had at least provided some structure. As we surveyed the raw text, we realized we had found simplicity on the near side of complexity: oversimplification. Now we had to pursue elegance.

So we called Chris Smith. A tall, soft-spoken man, Smith had taken an interest in the Bible's natural literature during his undergraduate studies at Harvard. He continued his research as he pursued his master's studies at Gordon-Conwell Theological Seminary and then through his PhD at Boston College. We had worked with him on a previous reader's Bible, and we knew we'd need his help to create this new edition.

Chris's work is based on the belief that books (not chapters or verses) are the fundamental building blocks of Scripture, and any exploration of the text needs to start by understanding the author's intentions behind each book: "who wrote them, and for what reason; what kind of writing they were; how they were put together; and what their central message was."[5] In order to understand the Bible, we need to zoom out from the verses and get acquainted with each book as a unified work, interacting with it holistically and on its own terms.

Like an archaeologist, Chris had spent years dusting away the artificial divisions of chapters and verses and discovering the various ways the original authors embedded signals of literary structure directly into each book. At one point in his career, he even taught a course called Smoke and Signals: "When you open the Bible, you get a lot of smoke blowing in your eyes, keeping you from seeing what's really there. But at the same time there are signals . . . that indicate what's going on."[6] Buried beneath the sand of the modern Bible, the real Bible's bones are still intact.

After years of research and reflection, Smith became convinced that the ancient authors often used repeated phrases to signal "seams" in their literature and give structure to their work. He cross-examined the phrases against each book's overall message, flow, and theme to make sure they weren't simply one of the author's favorite expressions. Time and time again, the phrases lined up with a change in genre, topical turning point, or plot progression.

His premise makes good sense. When the books were originally composed, the authors didn't have the luxury of the line spaces, headings, or chapter breaks that modern authors use to give structure to their work. Materials were expensive, so they wrote continuously, without spaces. And since the expectation was that these Scriptures would be read out loud to groups of listeners, the written appearance didn't matter much anyway.

The communities that first received these words would have been made up of attentive and careful listeners. Just as we're able to comprehend and retain complex information that we read and watch (at least, we were before the internet melted our brains), the ancients could process lengthy readings and speeches with their ears. They would have picked up on a phrase being used four or five or six times throughout the course of a book and understood it as a signal of a literary transition point. A couple of examples might be helpful.

The book of Acts is traditionally believed to have twenty-eight chapters, but it actually contains six natural sections. Acts tells the story of the first communities of Jesus' followers bringing the gospel message out of Jerusalem, encountering and overcoming significant barriers along the way. Each time a barrier is overcome and they advance the gospel, Luke uses a variation of "God's message continued to spread. The number of believers greatly increased" to mark a literary transition point. Here's an outline, with chapter and verse references if you want to look them up for yourself:

Phase 1: The message breaks through a linguistic barrier as the Jerusalem community welcomes Greek speakers. *(Acts 1:1–6:7)*

Phase 2: The message breaks through a geographic barrier as it spreads from Judea into Samaria. *(Acts 6:8–9:31)*

Phase 3: The community welcomes Gentiles, breaking through a significant ethnic/cultural barrier. *(Acts 9:32–12:24)*

Phase 4: Another geographic barrier is broken. The gospel moves into Asia Minor. *(Acts 12:25–16:5)*

Phase 5: The gospel moves into Greece, the cultural center of the ancient Mediterranean world. *(Acts 16:6–19:20)*

Phase 6: The message that Jesus is Lord and King arrives in Rome, right under the nose of Caesar. *(Acts 19:21–28:30)*

Luke's Gospel tells the story of Jesus' journey *toward* Jerusalem, where his mission and the Jewish story would come to their climax and where the decisive battle against the evil powers would be won. His second volume, Acts, tells the story of the Good News making its way *out from* Jerusalem, growing up from its Jewish roots into a message for the whole world. The literary form and content in Acts work together to communicate the same message: The gospel is for everyone. It's on the move. It won't be stopped.

Another great example is Matthew's Gospel, which also has twenty-eight chapters. Once we dust away the numbers, though, we find something much more interesting. Written to a Jewish audience, Matthew continually ties the life of Jesus to the story of Israel. His goal is to show that this crucified man from Nazareth is actually the King of the Jews, the long-awaited fulfillment of their hopes and dreams.

His portrayal of Jesus consistently echoes the life of Israel's first great rescuer, Moses. As a baby, Jesus escapes King Herod's plot to murder all the baby boys in Bethlehem, just as Moses had evaded Pharaoh's order to kill every newborn Hebrew boy. Moses spent forty years in the wilderness; Jesus goes out into the wilderness for forty days before beginning his ministry. And just as Moses went up a mountain to receive the law, Jesus climbs a mountain to announce what it means to participate in God's kingdom.

At every turn, Jesus is characterized as Moses 2.0. Moses was Israel's greatest teacher, prophet, and lawgiver—Jesus is greater in all three roles. He would not rescue his people merely from Egypt or Babylon or even Rome but from the deeper powers of sin and death, which give strength to every oppressor.

Structurally, Matthew is built upon five paired sections of narrative and teaching. After each one of Jesus' teachings, Matthew uses a variation of the phrase "When Jesus had finished saying these things . . ." to signal a transition to a new section. Each coupling of action and teaching reveals a different expression of God's renewal in the world, which Matthew calls "the kingdom of heaven." He wants us to see that God's kingdom is breaking in through the words, deeds, death, and resurrection of Jesus.

Prologue: Jesus' genealogy begins by declaring him as the *son* (descendant) *of David* and the *son of Abraham*, tying him definitively to the work God began through Israel. *(Matthew 1:1-16)*

Part 1: The foundations of the kingdom of heaven
(Matthew 1:17–7:29)

Part 2: The mission of the kingdom of heaven
(Matthew 8:1–10:42)

Part 3: The mystery of the kingdom of heaven
(Matthew 11:1–13:52)

Part 4: The family of the kingdom of heaven
(Matthew 13:53–18:35)

Part 5: The destiny of the kingdom of heaven
(Matthew 19:1–25:46)

Culmination: The story of Jesus establishing God's kingdom
through his victory on the cross *(Matthew 26:1–28:20)*

The five sections of Matthew are not coincidental. The book
is bending over backward to show that God has not abandoned
Israel, that his promises still stand. Jesus is indeed bringing the
nation's story to its climax. If Jesus is the new Moses, the five sections of this Gospel both echo and fulfill the five books of Moses:
Genesis, Exodus, Leviticus, Numbers, and Deuteronomy.

Bringing It All Together

At this point in our attempt to create an elegantly simple Bible-
reading experience, chapter numbers, verse numbers, and the rest
of the modern additives were gone. Poetry looked like poetry,
and letters looked like letters. Each book's natural literary structures were proudly displayed with line breaks and small graphical

markers. The Bible looked just as readable as Harry Potter. There was just one more piece to address: the books themselves.

When we studied the Bible's history, we discovered that some books had been artificially split up, simply because centuries ago they were too long to fit on a single scroll. So 1 and 2 Samuel and 1 and 2 Kings were all reunited as Samuel–Kings. We did the same with Israel's second history, Chronicles–Ezra–Nehemiah. If you look at the last two verses of 2 Chronicles and the first two verses of Ezra, you'll notice they repeat. The repetition isn't accidental—it's an intentional overlap from the days of scrolls indicating that the books are supposed to go together. Luke and Acts were put back together as Luke–Acts, volume 1 and volume 2 of Luke's account to Theophilus.

We also discovered that there's no divinely inspired order of books in the Bible. Before the printing press set our familiar order in stone, hand-copied Bibles organized the books in a variety of ways—sometimes chronologically, sometimes from longest to shortest. Sometimes the book order was based on the preferences of churches in different geographical regions. The only group of books that hasn't changed order is the first five books, Genesis through Deuteronomy. So we felt comfortable moving books around as we saw fit.

The most significant reshuffling came in the New Testament. Since our goal is for people to read cover to cover, the current New Testament book order makes little sense. All four Gospels are lumped together at the beginning, so if you start in Matthew, by the time you're midway through Luke you start feeling like Bill Murray in *Groundhog Day*. Paul's letters are traditionally arranged in order from longest (Romans) to shortest (Philemon), which isn't very helpful if you want to follow along with Paul's ministry and the development of his theology.

We built our New Testament book order upon the four pillars of the Gospel books and surrounded each Gospel with books that naturally correspond. We began with Luke–Acts, the story of Jesus and the story of the early church. Since Luke was a traveling companion of Paul, Paul's letters immediately follow in a more chronological order.

Mark's Gospel is next, followed by 1 and 2 Peter and Jude. According to church tradition, Mark was a close companion of Peter and likely used Peter's recollections of Jesus' life to shape his Gospel account. The premise of Jude's letter is very similar to that of Peter's letters.

Matthew is grouped with Hebrews and James because these three books all depict the gospel from a distinctly Jewish standpoint. Finally, John's Gospel is grouped with his three letters, and Revelation concludes the New Testament with a glimpse into the culmination of God's purposes for his creation—"a new heaven and a new earth."[7]

In 2018, these changes came together in *Immerse: The Reading Bible,* a six-volume edition of the Bible crafted to provide the best reading experience possible. We took all the changes I've described in this chapter and combined them with the science of reading-centered design, accounting for line length, paper thickness, spacing, margins, and a handful of other design principles to create the best possible conditions for a relaxed and enjoyable reading experience.

This new Bible format is paired with a new community experience around the text (which we'll explore more in chapter 5) that functions less like a typical Bible study and more like a book club.

According to many participants, the natural and intuitive formatting makes all the difference. "The narrative format of this allowed it to come alive for them," one pastor said of his congregation's experience. "And they have seen things they've not seen before—people who have read the Bible for *years*."[8]

Christian schools and universities have also started using Immerse in their Bible courses. Having students read a Bible that looks more like a novel gives teachers the perfect tool to take them through large portions of Scripture and have them experience it in a new way. "The verses, the chapters . . . the headings and everything . . . the notes— it's . . . distracting," said one college student. "But with Immerse, it's like one big story—it's like I'm reading an actual book."[9]

Freedom

In the 1980s, a team of art-restoration experts walked into the Sistine Chapel and began a massive, multiyear project to restore the ceiling's artwork. Their goal was to use a laboratory-tested solvent to wash away the soot and grime and also remove the layers of other substances earlier conservators had used to protect the ceiling. They wanted to get back to the original paint laid in the early 1500s and then cover it with a thin, clear layer of modern protective chemicals.

As they slowly dissolved the layers of buildup, it was as if dawn had finally broken after centuries of twilight. Hidden beneath the dirt, grit, and crust was Michelangelo's original work. Bright, vibrant colors jumped off the walls—deep violets, brilliant blues, strong reds. "It is like opening a window in a dark room and seeing it flooded with light," wrote Carlo Pietrangeli, former Director General of the

Vatican Museums. Art scholar John Osborne declared that "every book on Michelangelo [would] have to be rewritten."[10]

There is freedom in recovering something that has been lost over time. We need to recover a form of the Bible that is not only easier to read but also aligns with what the Bible actually *is*.

Shortly after Immerse was launched, word got around to a church operating within Ionia Correctional Facility, a maximum-security prison in western Michigan. The small-group book-club model appealed to them, so they decided to split their three-hundred-inmate congregation into thirty small groups and give it a try.

Before starting with the whole congregation, the thirty small group leaders spent two weeks reading this new Bible to prepare themselves to lead their groups. When the trial period was over, they invited one of my colleagues, Paul Caminiti, to visit the facility to talk about the rationale behind this new way of reading the Bible.

Paul gave a short presentation about the thinking that went into the formatting, plus a little background on the book-club discussion model. Then he spent over an hour simply chatting with the men. They sat in folding chairs arranged in a circle and talked about their experience reading this new Bible format. Every one of them had something to say.

At one point, a middle-aged, African American man spoke up. "Every moment of our days in here is regulated," he said. "When we get out of bed, when we eat, when we exercise, when we go to sleep at night." He paused. "Since I've been in here, I've had a lot of time on my hands to read the Bible. But it wasn't until I started reading this particular Bible that I realized how chapters and verses have been regulating the text. *Now it feels like the text has been set free.*"

practices

PART TWO

Read Big

Normalization creates culture, and culture drives our choices,
which leads to more normalization.
SETH GODIN

IF YOU WANT TO HAVE A RICHER, more meaningful, more enjoyable experience reading the Bible, simply using a reader's Bible will go a long way. The different format will naturally guide you toward better practices. That said, old habits die hard. If you try to fit your old ways of reading into this new format, you'll realize they don't align very well.

Over the next few chapters we're going to examine some of the most pervasive bad habits of Bible reading, which often come baked into modern Christianity in the West, and I'll suggest some new habits that will help you experience the Bible coming alive in new and refreshing ways.

For starters, we need to talk about our obsession with reading small.

When I was a kid, one of my favorite restaurants was Old Country Buffet. Tucked back in the corner of a local shopping center, between a movie theater and a dry cleaner's, it was the site of more than a few birthday-celebration dinners in our family. I looked it up recently and saw that it had permanently closed, finishing with an average customer rating of two stars.

As I recall, there was no menu. My parents paid the price of admission, and we were unleashed into the carnival of all-you-can-eat buffet lines like a pack of hyenas. It wasn't uncommon to return to our table with a plate of fried chicken, mac 'n' cheese, pizza, corn dogs, and Jell-O haphazardly piled on top of one another like a junkyard of fat, sugar, and carbs. The salad bar was avoided.

The autonomy to pick and choose as we pleased was intoxicating. Unconstrained by the typical conventions of a meal, we were free to focus on our favorites. If we wanted to construct a cobbler/ice cream/brownie/cookie/marshmallow tower for dessert, we were well within our rights to do so.

Now that I'm older, I see a lot of parallels between the mindset my siblings and I brought to Old Country Buffet and the pick-and-choose mindset that has deeply shaped the Bible-reading practices of many Christians in America.

Beginning in Sunday school, kids are introduced to the Bible as an anthology of isolated stories, each with a moral or spiritual lesson attached. They're given a memory verse to take home and incentivized with a prize to recite it the next week. In some ways, it makes good sense to start children with these bite-size, easily digestible bits of Scripture. There's a lot in the Bible that they're not ready for yet. The problem is that most of us never graduate from this style of reading.

As we get older, we get busier. Responsibilities pile up and free time shrinks. As we explored in chapter 2, the sheer amount of information we're exposed to in a given day (roughly thirty-four gigabytes, if you recall) forces us into a system of "insidious trade-off between our need to know [and] our need to save and gain time," says Maryanne Wolf in *Reader, Come Home*. "Sometimes we outsource our intelligence to the information outlets that offer the fastest, simplest, most digestible distillations of information we no longer want to think about ourselves."[1]

And so, aided and encouraged by our fragmented modern Bibles, we continue to consume the Bible piecemeal, the way we were taught as children. "Many of us have read the Bible as if it were merely a mosaic of little bits—theological bits, moral bits, historical-critical bits, sermon bits, devotional bits,"[2] say Bible scholars Craig Bartholomew and Michael Goheen. We want the Bible to speak to us, but frankly, we don't have time to wade through any of the parts that don't feel immediately relevant. We're drawn to the autonomy of the Bible buffet.

Thus, most of the Bible is eliminated from consideration. Ancient battles with Amalekites, lengthy genealogies of obscure tribes, detailed instructions for wave offerings and drink offerings, correspondence about circumcision—it's hard to see how any of this could be helpful for making it through day-to-day life in the twenty-first century.

Our goal becomes fitting the Bible into our busy lives, and the easiest way to do that is by minimizing it, chopping it up, and ignoring the majority of it. We subsist on a diet of curated fragments, often taken out of context, that cut through the extracurricular Bible clutter and seem to speak directly into modern life. "The modern church has created an entire *culture* around Bible McNuggets," Philip Yancey once said, "and assumed they were nutritious."[3]

By limiting our engagement to cherry-picked fragments useful for personal application, we make the Bible subject to our agendas, our circumstances, and our feelings. Eugene Peterson says it this way:

> We are in the odd and embarrassing position of being a church in which many among us believe ardently in the authority of the Bible but, instead of submitting to it, use it, apply it, take charge of it endlessly, using our own experience as the authority for how and where and when we will use it.[4]

The Bible becomes small because we make it small. It loses its power to transcend our circumstances because we force it into *merely* addressing our circumstances.

The Bible will still speak into our lives—more powerfully, in fact, than we may be used to. But we need to give up control over it. We need to abandon the shortcuts we've relied on and settle in for a longer, slower journey through the Scriptures. It's the journey that will form us.

So how do we leave the Bible buffet and begin receiving the Bible—the whole Bible—on its own terms? It's pretty simple, really. First, we read whole books.

Reading Big

We read whole books because they, not chapters or verses, are the actual building blocks of God's redemptive story told throughout

Scripture. Books and their various authors, genres, cultural settings, and historical moments are how God chose to give the gift of the Bible to us. Receiving this gift means adapting our habits to interact with it on its own terms.

So jump in. Don't overthink it—pick a book and read it from start to finish. Narrative books like the Gospels, Acts, Esther, or Ruth may be easiest to start with. Or you can pick one of Paul's letters and read the whole thing from start to finish like you'd read any other letter. Besides Romans and the letters to the Corinthians, each can be read in under twenty minutes.

As you read, you'll encounter familiar stories and well-worn verses in their natural habitats. You'll read the lesser-known in-between stories that knit the famous ones together. And you'll inevitably come across things you had no idea were in the Bible. Things will get reframed within the overarching mission of the book, and you'll notice yourself molding to the author's agenda and getting swept up in their story rather than forcing them into yours. Reading big invites us to step back from the trees in order to see the grandeur of the forest.

Reading Fast and Slow

Reading big is simultaneously a fast and slow process.

Fast because we move through each book intentionally, resisting the tendency to get bogged down in the weeds. Now that we're using a reader's Bible, we no longer have chapter breaks that offer us an easy exit, so we just keep going. Speed is not necessarily the goal, and we don't need to commit to finishing a whole book in one sitting (although forty of the Bible's books can each be read in under an hour), but remember, we're trying to get a sense of the landscape.

So rid yourself of the pressure to extract every ounce of information. Don't worry so much about application. Instead of asking, *What is God saying to me?*, simply ask, *What is God saying? What is he up to? What is happening here?*

As you cultivate the practice of repeatedly engaging with whole books, the words you're reading will become well-trodden ground. You'll be back in these woods again, ready to read a bit more slowly and with a bit more depth. So relax your white-knuckled grip on the Bible and turn your hands to an open posture of reception. Let the text simply wash over you. These words have power in them. Read. Listen. Absorb.

This way of reading is *slow* because it requires patience and the slightly heroic act of surrendering more time and attention than you may be used to. While the Bible is certainly written *for* us, it was not written *to* us. It's a compilation of someone else's stories, someone else's mail, someone else's diary entries, someone else's problems. It's the story of how God has worked over time, through real people and real situations, to move his purposes forward.

So we need to follow Dallas Willard's advice to "ruthlessly eliminate hurry."[5] We need to eliminate the hurry for the Bible to speak directly to me, feed me, and address my problems and circumstances. We need to set our personal agendas aside and instead immerse ourselves in the roller-coaster sagas of God's ancient people—their dilemmas, struggles, triumphs, and celebrations. Oftentimes, there simply won't be a "personal takeaway." We won't find the instant gratification we may be used to from a "Fifteen Verses for Encouragement" list.

But the payoff will come. Reading this way is an act of trust in the Bible's divine Author. When we continually read big and without an agenda, we allow the words to soak into our bones without necessarily knowing what use they'll be to us. This is the formation process. And when any number of situations arise, we'll have more than just a verse or two to hang our hats upon. Richness will spring forth from unexpected places as we recall parallels between our modern lives and their ancient ones, knowing that the same God who was there then is here now.

Literacy and Fluency

I've noticed that as pastors and Christian leaders talk about the importance of reading the Bible, they almost always tout Bible literacy as the ultimate goal. Literacy is important, sure, but I think it's actually a prerequisite step on the journey toward our true goal: fluency. Literacy equips us with a baseline understanding of the facts and the vocabulary; fluency happens when we become intimately familiar with the Bible.

If you've ever attempted to learn a foreign language, you've experienced the chasm between literacy and fluency. I took German from eighth through twelfth grade, spending endless hours in the classroom memorizing vocabulary and conjugating verbs. By the time I was a graduating senior, I could stammer through a short, simple conversation around a very narrow topic. After five years, the language still felt, well, foreign. Putting sentences together felt clunky and unfamiliar. I was somewhat literate but far from fluent.

Things would have been much different, of course, if I had moved to Germany for a few years and completely immersed myself in the language and culture. Fluency often happens through the passive absorption that comes from being immersed in something for a period of time.

Reading whole books orients us toward the pursuit of biblical fluency. We read and we reread not so much to memorize and systematize but to cultivate a deep familiarity with the text. Memorizing verses is great (as long as it's done in context), but what if we could spontaneously speak off the cuff about Jesus' teachings from the Sermon on the Mount? What if we could give an overview from memory of the life of Jacob or the story of Ruth, not necessarily because we had memorized them word for word but because we'd spent enough time simply reading them to become conversant? That's what Bible fluency is all about.

The Bible-Reading Ecosystem

You may be thinking, *What about Bible study? What about daily readings, like lectionaries or the Daily Office, or meditative reading, like Lectio Divina?* To be sure, there are many Bible-engagement practices on the spectrum between the minimalistic, buffet-style reading I described at the beginning of the chapter and the long-form reading I've outlined. Where do they fit in the Bible-engagement equation?

First, let's talk about Bible study. At some point along the way, study overtook reading as the primary thing to do with the Scriptures. The format of our modern Bibles, our modern tendency to dissect and analyze, and the erosion of long-form reading in our culture have all pushed us toward microscopic examination of the text and away from telescopic exploration.

Even new believers, who have just accepted Jesus, are often handed their first Bible (a completely foreign object) and instructed to study it. No mention of reading. Christians who want to get serious about Scripture buy a study Bible chock-full of thousands of study notes and so huge it can prop their car up during an oil change. Study, study, study. That's the key.

Here's the thing: Bible study is a good and important exercise to deepen our understanding of God and grow our faith. There's a place in the Bible-engagement ecosystem for honing in on a section or paragraph or sentence or word and digging into it. Tracing a theme through the Bible can be immensely enlightening. But these are all secondary exercises.

Before we can dig deep, we need to read big. Study will only be aided by big-picture understandings of how whole books work, how groups of books function, and how the Bible's story fits together as a whole. So rather than thinking of study as the first (and sometimes only) thing to do with the Bible, we should use it to complement the primary practice of reading. We should move back and forth between these two important practices, using one to enrich the other.

Meditative reading practices like Lectio Divina also provide important and powerful avenues for connecting with God through the Scriptures. Lectio Divina invites us to read a short passage slowly and carefully, listening for a word or phrase that the Spirit is highlighting. We sit with that passage or that word, turning it over in our souls and listening for what God may be saying to us. We reread the passage a few more times, taking time to pray, reflect, meditate, and contemplate.

The body of Christ has employed practices like these for

centuries. They help us acknowledge that the words of the Bible are truly living and allow us to make space for the Spirit to speak to us.

But again, these practices only become more effective when they take place in tandem with the consistent habit of reading big. Becoming fluent in the big picture gives us an important backdrop for meditating on the small parts.

Finally, many liturgical traditions use resources like the Daily Office or other lectionary readers to invite Christians into Scripture on a daily basis. These scheduled readings often go through books of the Bible from start to finish, which is much better than randomly jumping around like many devotional materials do. The problem is that the reading schedules typically move *slowly*, taking readers along at a pace of just a handful of verses a day.

Imagine settling in to watch a movie. It's Friday night, you've got your buttery popcorn and your drink of choice. You press Play, and the main character flashes up on the screen. As she starts her day—hurrying through breakfast, brushing her teeth, hustling down the crowded streets of Manhattan in a suit and heels with a cup of coffee in hand—questions begin to swirl in your mind. *Who is she? Where does she work? What problems is she going to face?*

You watch for ten minutes or so, then pause the movie, turn off the TV, and head to bed. "I'll pick up here tomorrow," you say. You watch for ten minutes the next day. And the day after that. A couple of weeks later you finally finish the movie.

Crazy, right? Except this is what we often do with the Bible. Reading Scripture daily is great, but if we only ever read in fits and starts, it's impossible to get immersed in the text. We lose any sense of continuity and flow, which can easily turn any good story into a complete bore. As a friend of mine likes to say, "reading a page a day will make anything the worst read of your life."

So what does a healthy Bible-engagement ecosystem look like? Clearly, long-form reading is not meant to sweep everything else off the table and become our exclusive means of getting into the Word. But the first and most natural thing to do with the Bible is to read whole books and whole literary units as the groundwork for all the other complementary reading practices.

Strange New World

In 1916, a young pastor named Karl Barth gave an address in Leutwil, a Swiss village near the French and German borders. The two neighboring nations, and indeed most of Europe, were mired in World War I, tangled up in death and destruction on a scale the world had never seen. Although Switzerland was neutral, its people were not unaffected by the war. Surrounded by carnage, with everyone anxiously listening for news from the front, Barth interjected with a question to the Leutwil congregation: *What is there within the Bible?*

"What is the significance of the remarkable line from Abraham to Christ? What of the chorus of the prophets and apostles? and what is the burden of their song? What is the one truth that these voices evidently all desire to announce, each in its own tone, each in its own way?"[6]

Barth warns that if we come looking for a certain kind of answer for what's in the Bible, we will likely find it. If we want high and divine content barely connected to the grit and dust of the earth, that is what we'll see. If we want to simply read the Bible as the fleeting historical documents of an ancient people, we'll find that, too. And if we believe the Bible has nothing to offer us, then it could very well fulfill our expectations. These pages can become a mirror, reflecting our desires and agendas back upon us.

Asking the question *What is there within the Bible?* requires moving beyond ourselves, trusting God as we "reach eagerly for an answer which is really much too large for us, for which we really are not yet ready, and of which we do not seem worthy."[7]

Barth suggests an answer. The chorus of voices and events in these pages bear witness: "Within the Bible there is a strange, new world, the world of God."[8]

> See, I am doing a new thing!
>> Now it springs up; do you not perceive it?
> I am making a way in the wilderness
>> and streams in the wasteland.

THE PROPHET ISAIAH[9]

The Bible's story takes place within real history, yet it is unbound by the normal conventions of mere history. It defies our expectations, upends our agendas, perplexes us, confounds us. Because God lives, acts, and speaks, a "history with its own distinct grounds, possibilities, and hypotheses"[10] emerges.

We find that there's no neat and tidy way to read the Bible as a curriculum for a life well lived. Interspersed with heroic stories of virtue are tales of horrific violence and immorality, not to mention all the parts that seem totally foreign and irrelevant. If we come to the Bible as a mere guidebook for life, we'll often be met with confusion and disappointment. "Time and time again the Bible gives us the impression that it contains no instructions, counsels, or examples whatsoever, either for individuals or for nations and governments; and the impression is correct. It offers us not at all what we first seek in it."[11]

So what does it mean for the Bible to be *for* us? It means immersing ourselves in the pages of this book and seeing that God is planting seeds for a new thing, inviting us into something distinctly Other in the midst of the carnage of war, the frustration of politics, and the mundaneness of everyday life. "One cannot learn or imitate this life of the divine seed in the new world. One can only let it live, grow, and ripen within him."[12]

It means turning from our temptation to take the easy way out and cherry-pick the easily applicable golden nuggets. It means reading big, reading whole books, and opening ourselves up to *everything* God has to say. Along the way, we will certainly find takeaways, guidance, and truth we can bring into our lives. But reading the Bible means first and foremost being drawn into its reality, participating with God on his terms.

"There is a river in the Bible that carries us away, once we have entrusted our destiny to it," says Barth, "away from ourselves to the sea."[13]

Read Together

It is a myth of Western, modernist, and particularly American thinking
that we can or should be Lone Ranger readers.
JEANNINE K. BROWN

"UM. WHERE'S Jesus?"

Every parent knows that feeling—that sinking sense of panic that takes over when they've lost track of their kid. Luke's Gospel tells the story of Mary, Joseph, and Jesus traveling to Jerusalem for the Passover festival and, once the feast days have ended, packing up and beginning the journey back home. After a full day of travel, Jesus' parents realize that their twelve-year-old is not, in fact, among their friends and relatives somewhere else in the caravan.

They hurry back to Jerusalem and scour the city. After three days of searching for him, they find him at the Temple, "sitting among the teachers, listening to them and asking them questions. Everyone who heard him was astonished at his understanding and his answers."[1]

Mary, however, is not impressed. The reader can almost see her grabbing the boy Jesus' face in both hands, her bloodshot eyes boring into him. "Young man, why have you done this to us? Your father and I have been half out of our minds looking for you."[2]

Jesus replies, "Why were you looking for me? Didn't you know that I would have to be getting involved with my father's work?"[3]

Now that I have a five-year-old and a three-year-old, I've gained a new level of sympathy for Mary and Joseph in this story. But I've also been struck by the matter-of-factness of Jesus' response. Despite his parents' fervor, it's obvious to Jesus that he had to stay behind. On the cusp of adulthood, which would come at age thirteen, Jesus is preparing to be a full participant in the Jewish synagogue. He understands that his "father's work" and a key part of his ministry to come is a commitment to ongoing community immersion in the Scriptures.

The Synagogue in Jewish Life

Although the exact origins of the synagogue are a bit murky, it's commonly believed that it grew out of Israel's return from the Babylonian exile. Around 538 BC the nation limped back to Jerusalem battered, bruised, and demoralized from seventy years of captivity. Their once glorious city was now reduced to ashes and rubble. As they began the arduous work of rebuilding their home, deep questions lingered: *Who are we? Is God still with us? Where is our story going?* No amount of stone and mortar was going to fix their shattered identity.

Then something surprising happened. The people came to Ezra the priest with a request. "In October, when the Israelites had settled in their towns, all the people assembled with a unified purpose at the square just inside the Water Gate. They asked Ezra the scribe to bring out the Book of the Law of Moses, which the LORD had given for Israel to obey."[4]

They constructed a large wooden platform for Ezra to stand on and speak from, and all the men, women, and children old enough to understand gathered to listen. Ezra read aloud from the Torah for hours at a time, with the Levites spread out among the crowd to help them understand the meaning of each passage. Many people wept as they heard their long-forgotten Scriptures read aloud. They were reminded of their founding story, their calling as a holy nation, and how far they had strayed from it.

This pivotal event launched a recommitment to the Scriptures throughout Israel. Among other things, the nation established synagogues as gathering places committed to ongoing community immersion in the sacred texts. By the first century, every city and village had a synagogue, which, in addition to the weekly Sabbath worship gatherings, served as a multipurpose community center for shared meals, charitable activities, and education.

The Sabbath gatherings typically consisted of prayer, Scripture reading, a teaching or explanation, and open discussion. Although there were synagogue leaders, these events were unmistakably community oriented. Even the architecture of some early synagogues was geared toward group interaction: The place where the teacher would stand to read (and sit to teach) was situated in the center of the room instead of at the front, and the seats were arranged to face the teacher.

"This architectural layout is designed for discussion," explains Jordan J. Ryan. "In particular, the quadrilateral seating arrangement facilitates discussion, especially between people seated on opposite sides of the assembly hall as well as with anyone in the open central area. This would have allowed congregants to easily engage anyone speaking in the centre or sitting opposite from them in debate or discussion."[5]

In the Gospels, significant portions of Jesus' ministry take place in synagogues. Luke recounts Jesus returning to Galilee, filled with the Holy Spirit after enduring Satan's temptations in the wilderness: "He taught regularly in their synagogues and was praised by everyone."[6] On the day he launches his ministry with a reading from Isaiah, the scene is introduced like this: "When he came to the village of Nazareth, his boyhood home, he went *as usual* to the synagogue on the Sabbath and stood up to read the Scriptures."[7] Jesus makes a point of going to the places where the Scriptures are being routinely heard and discussed to announce and demonstrate that they are being fulfilled in him.

After his resurrection and ascension, his followers do the same. Acts describes Paul entering the synagogue in Thessalonica, "and on three Sabbath days he reasoned with them from the Scriptures, explaining and proving that the Messiah had to suffer and rise from the dead."[8] Paul and Barnabas preach a similar message at the synagogue in Pisidian Antioch, and the conversation actually spills out into the streets afterward. The gospel of Jesus the Messiah was tied to the corporate story and communal identity of the Jews found in their Scriptures. The Good News was good, in part, because it meant that God had kept his promises—promises that the Jewish people had been reading, interpreting, and anticipating together for centuries.

As the first Christian communities began gathering, they

inherited many elements of the Jewish synagogue. Paul instructs Timothy to devote himself "to the public reading of Scripture, to preaching and to teaching."[9] Second-century church father Justin Martyr describes the community's Sunday gatherings, where "all who live in cities or in the country gather together to one place, and the memoirs of the apostles or the writings of the prophets are read, as long as time permits."[10]

The Challenge of Reading Alone

Contrast all this with the privatized and individualized Bible reading that has become the norm today. Saturated in the individualism that arose from the European Enlightenment, we no longer think of ourselves primarily as a part of a group or community but as individual agents with the autonomy to make our own way in the world. "You can steer yourself any direction you choose," says Dr. Seuss in the wildly popular *Oh, the Places You'll Go!*, often given as a graduation present. "You're on your own. And you know what you know. And *YOU* are the guy who'll decide where to go."[11]

Equipped with our very own Bibles and empowered by the Reformation's reminder that the church is a priesthood of believers, we feel completely validated reading and interpreting our Bibles *alone*. In private. Me, the Spirit, and a hot cup of coffee.

Personal devotions and quiet times have taken over our collective imagination and provided a singular image of what good Bible reading looks like. And while these private habits of reading, prayer, and communion with God are indeed precious and important, we rarely stop to consider what is lost when they become our exclusive means of engaging with the Word. What goes missing when we only read the Bible isolated from the rest of the body of Christ? What can we recover by gathering back together around the text?

First off, for many people, the formation of a Bible-reading habit doesn't actually happen at all. Every January, multitudes of Christians pull out their read-the-Bible-in-a-year plan (a much too ambitious schedule, in my opinion, but that's a different discussion) and assure themselves that this is going to be the year they buckle down and make it happen. By February, they're lost in the Bermuda Triangle of Leviticus, Numbers, and Deuteronomy and, well, we all know how that goes. Using a reader's Bible and reading big can help with this, but many people still have trouble spending consistent time in Scripture without the support and accountability of a community that is reading and reflecting with them.

As Christian leaders frantically try to address plummeting Bible-reading rates, their proposed solutions hinge on individual habit formation: carve out a consistent time of day to read, pray for a hunger for the Word, try using a journal. As far as I can tell, their tips and tricks are falling flat. Bootstrapping and self-discipline might be woven into the fabric of American idealism, but they're not doing much to move the needle when it comes to Bible reading.

Shortly after I moved to Colorado, I joined a book club and learned the value of positive social pressure. We half jokingly call ourselves the Ents (after the tree-people from The Lord of the Rings, who famously talk at a glacial pace) because it takes us forever to get through any given book.

Despite the slow pace, I usually struggle to keep up with the reading. The books we choose are almost always dense books on theology or biblical studies, and while I consider myself a decent armchair theologian, these are not the types of books I'd take to the beach for a leisurely read. But since I'm part of the group, I'm much more disciplined about reading the assigned pages than I otherwise would be. I know that on Friday morning I'm expected to show up at Panera, overpay for a mediocre breakfast, and join the Ents for a discussion.

Study after study affirms the power a network of friends can have on habit formation and behavior change, yet millions of Christians struggle to form a sustainable Bible-reading practice because they're under the impression that they're on their own.

Second, by reading alone we naturally look through a lens of individualistic interpretation. We read the Bible's promises as promises *to me* and commands as commands *for me* (a habit that becomes even worse when we only read selected bits and pieces, ignoring the huge portions of Scripture that couldn't possibly fit those expectations). Most private devotions end with questions aimed at personal application—an inwardly focused practice that encourages readers to ponder their own thoughts on a Bible passage for the rest of the day.

This is okay as far as it goes. God certainly cares deeply about each of us and wants to form us as individuals. But by its very nature, the Bible is a book written to communities, for communities, originally read aloud and heard by groups. The word *you* in the Bible is often plural, more like *y'all*. By only ever reading the Bible as a private conversation between ourselves and God, we end up out of sync with the Bible's primary mission.

"Wherever you go in the Bible, it is the same: the work of God is *to form a community* in which the will of God is done and through which one finds both union with God and communion with others for the good of others and the world," says New Testament scholar Scot McKnight.[12] As much as individualism has soaked through Western—particularly American—culture, the Christian race is not meant to be run alone. "Scripture is the Spirit-inspired story of Jesus as communicated through, to, and for the church."[13]

Finally, privatized Bible reading robs us of the collective wisdom of the community. Modern individualism has crafted a myth that tells us reading alone is the only way to stay on the path to true understanding. The nineteenth-century evangelist Charles Finney wrote, "I found myself utterly unable to accept doctrine on the ground of authority. . . . I had nowhere to go but directly to the Bible, and to the philosophy or workings of my own mind. I gradually formed a view of my own . . . which appeared to me to be unequivocally taught in the Bible."[14]

This Lone Ranger approach mistakenly assumes that any of us can come to the Bible as a blank slate, but the reality is that all of us read the text from within our own context. We've all been shaped in ten thousand different ways by our families, church communities, traditions, and personal experiences. We bring our whole selves to the Bible, filtering it through the many layers of who we are.

The Scriptures are certainly meant to speak to us in the midst of real life, but the baggage we bring to our Bible reading means that each of us has our own set of blind spots, and the nature of blind spots is that *we can't see them.*

In *Reading While Black: African American Biblical Interpretation as an Exercise in Hope,* Esau McCaulley argues that although we all read from the same Bible, our backgrounds and biases naturally lead us to elevate some passages over others. "All theology is canonical in that everyone who attempts to think about the Bible must place the variety of biblical texts in some kind of order, understanding one in light of others. This isn't unique to Black Christians; everyone does it. The question isn't always which account of Christianity uses the Bible. The question is which does justice to as much of the biblical witness as possible."[15]

It does us no favors to stay locked inside the echo chambers of our own thoughts, traditions, and experiences. We need our perspectives to be challenged and refined by others, who bring a different set of lenses to their reading of the text, all with the goal of doing more justice to the entirety of the biblical witness. As a white American male, I need to intentionally pursue the perspectives of people who *aren't like me*. I need to read and discuss Scripture with people who look different from me, who grew up in different places, who have endured different challenges, who identify with different passages and characters than I do. I need to learn from people who can shed light on parts of the Bible I've never noticed before.

Now, this isn't to say we should slide into some sort of relativism where the Bible's truth and meaning are defined by our experiences—you have your truth, and I have mine. My point is that none of us has cornered the market on understanding. The family of God is a global, multicultural, multigenerational mosaic. We need to work together to balance one another's perspectives, expand one another's vision, and reveal one another's blind spots.

By reading alone, cloistered away from the wisdom of the community, none of that is possible.

Recovering Textual Communities

So what could it look like to begin recovering the textual communities of the ancient synagogue and the early church? Here are three things you and your community can pursue to begin working back toward communal reading, interpretation, and application of the Bible.

1. Recover the public reading and hearing of Scripture.

One of the oldest and richest activities of the people of God has faded into the background of most modern church services. If there's any Scripture reading at all, it's often a brief and unrehearsed launchpad for the sermon. Sometimes the church service is devoid of any Bible text except for a verse inserted here or there to prop up the pastor's message.

We can bring Scripture back into the center of our Sunday gatherings. We can lobby the leadership of our churches to give Bible reading a place of prominence and train people within the church body to read the Scriptures aloud with beauty, clarity, and power. Bible reading doesn't have to be an uninspired pivot point between singing and sermon. We can create a culture within our churches where we intentionally lean in to hear Scripture read aloud for its own sake.

Aside from in our Sunday services, there are plenty of other ways to engage with the Word read aloud. An organization in New York City called The Public Reading of Scripture hosts open-invitation gatherings every week on the fortieth floor of the *New York Times* building. People from every walk of life congregate in a boardroom overlooking the bustling streets of Manhattan and simply listen to an audio recording of the Bible for an entire hour. While it may sound like a long and tedious activity to some of us, something happens in that room that keeps the Armani-wearing businessmen and the hot dog vendors coming back for more.

Other small groups have adopted "popcorn" reading, gathering together to read out loud for as long as time allows. Whoever wants to read can read for however long they want, and once they're finished, another person picks up where they left off. They usually aim to finish an entire book of the Bible in one gathering, or at least a major portion if it's one of the longer books.

As somebody who loves to learn and understand, I'm as guilty as anyone of tuning out public Scripture reading as I wait expectantly for the sermon or lesson. But the Old and New Testaments both bear witness to the power carried forth by Scripture when it washes over a community that has gathered to read and listen together.

2. Recover free-flowing discussions.

Here in Colorado Springs, our famous Garden of the Gods park is threaded with a network of hiking trails that weave through the towering red rock formations. Since it's such a popular tourist destination, the trails are dotted with signs urging visitors to Please Stay on the Trail. Above the message is a picture of a coiled rattlesnake, fangs bared and ready to strike.

If we're honest, "Please stay on the trail" could be the message used to introduce the typical Christian Bible study. The workbooks and DVDs often simply lead us on a guided tour through the text, periodically asking us to regurgitate a verse here or there in order to answer the predetermined discussion questions. The

Bible is a wild and scandalous book, yet the standard Bible study is boring, tame, and predictable. What could it look like for us to veer off-trail for an unmediated exploration of the Bible in all its strangeness and wonder?

The model is pretty simple: just read and then talk about it. Some groups read aloud together and then talk; others read at home and then gather together like a book club to discuss what they've read. Whatever you decide to do, keep the conversation open and honest. Talk about what you noticed for the first time, what you liked, what you didn't like, and what made no sense at all.

For Immerse groups, participants read anywhere from twenty-five to fifty pages at home during the week and then gather together for discussion. We encourage anyone with burning questions or observations to open the discussion by sharing with the group. If nobody has anything pressing to share, we suggest four conversation starters:

- What stood out to you this week?
- Was there anything confusing or troubling?
- Did anything make you think differently about God?
- How might this change the way we live?

By shifting the model from a predetermined formula to an organic conversation, our communities are invited to rummage through the Bible that's really there. Discussions are more focused on impressions of the text than on right or wrong answers. We can voice the questions, doubts, and struggles we are facing but perhaps have never felt comfortable sharing before. The Spirit has space to move as we laugh, cry, wrestle, and celebrate "Aha!" moments together.

Just like the trails in the Garden of the Gods, our groups will indeed encounter rattlesnakes once we abandon the safety of the path. There are plenty of hard parts of Scripture, but it's better to be honest about them than to pretend they don't exist. Sometimes the most comforting thing a struggling Christian can hear is "I don't know either." It's better for us to wrestle with the Bible together, turning it over and looking at it from our various perspectives, than to continue struggling alone.

I once heard a story about a woman who was invited to join a group that was reading through the entire New Testament and discussing it like a book club. She had never really read the Bible before. During one conversation, after the group had finished reading a few of Paul's epistles, she spoke up: "You all know I'm new at this. But I have to admit that when it comes to this Paul guy, I can't say I'm much of a fan. He seems like a bully."

What a great discussion it must have sparked! How often do new believers or those on the outskirts of faith get invited to a Bible study where everyone seems put together and sure of themselves as they confidently answer the prescribed questions? Setting the table for an "anything goes" conversation gives new believers a way to voice their questions without feeling stupid, and it gives longtime Christians the chance to share their struggles and doubts without feeling judged.

After the group had finished reading Paul's letters (arranged in chronological order) they asked the woman if her opinion had changed. She thought for a moment and said, "You know, I think he grew on me. He seemed to soften as time passed."

Paul writes in Ephesians, "I pray that you, being rooted and established in love, may have power, *together with all the Lord's holy people*, to grasp how wide and long and high and deep is the love of Christ."[16] Recovering organic discussions around the text will not only draw us deeper into Scripture, it will knit us more closely together. Talking openly and honestly about Scripture will often turn into talking openly and honestly about our own walks with God. There will inevitably be places where we don't see eye to eye, and we'll need to learn to manage disagreement with love and grace. Together, gathered around the entirety of our founding story told in the Bible, we can deepen our love of Christ and our love for one another.

3. Recover community application: What does this mean for us?

Inside each copy of *Immerse: The Reading Bible* is a bookmark containing the reading plan and the four discussion questions mentioned above. When we were in the final design stages for Immerse, a couple of days before all the files were going to be sent to the printer for the first twenty thousand–copy print run, I got an email.

It was a courtesy email from our publisher's design team. They had attached the design files for all the printed materials, including the bookmarks, for me to take a final look. As I scanned over the sentences I had already read twenty times before, something caught my attention, and my eyes bugged out. The final discussion question had been changed.

One of the editors had made a slight tweak to the question, phrasing it as "How might this change the way you live?" I fired back an email as quickly as I could: "Please change it back to 'the way *we* live'!!"

His mistake was completely understandable—the other three

questions were focused on individual impressions of the text—but one of the curveballs we intentionally threw into the group experience was an emphasis on *community* application.

We've been trained repeatedly by sermons, Sunday school classes, and Bible study materials to think of personal application as the ultimate endgame for any interaction with the Bible. But if the Bible is primarily a community-formation book, then insisting on only enacting its message through the narrow scope of my personal journey with Christ does a disservice to God's intentions for the text.

Instead, we have the opportunity to begin asking community-application questions. If we're reading the text together and having free-flowing, organic conversations, what if we peeled away an extra layer from our ingrained individualism and began thinking about how *we* can apply what we've read together?

Take Paul's famous spiritual warfare illustration in Ephesians as an example:

> Therefore, put on every piece of God's armor so you
> will be able to resist the enemy in the time of evil. Then
> after the battle you will still be standing firm. Stand your
> ground, putting on the belt of truth and the body armor
> of God's righteousness. For shoes, put on the peace that
> comes from the Good News so that you will be fully
> prepared. In addition to all of these, hold up the shield of
> faith to stop the fiery arrows of the devil. Put on salvation
> as your helmet, and take the sword of the Spirit, which is
> the word of God.[17]

We typically read this passage as instructions for putting on our own personal armor in preparation for the fight against the enemy's attacks on our private lives, and it can certainly still be read and applied that way. But if Paul wrote this letter to a church, what might it look like for an entire community to also work on applying this together? How can we assure that *together* we're wearing the belt of truth or the shoes of peace? Asking these questions and corporately resolving to live faithfully introduces support, interdependence, and accountability into our life together—three things our Christian communities are sorely lacking today.

It may not be possible to completely abandon the individualism we've been born and raised in, but we need to fight against the notion that the Christian community—the *ekklēsia*—is merely a smattering of individuals loosely connected by a shared belief system. If we truly believe we are all part of Christ's *body* (think about that word literally for a minute), each with our own gifts, roles, and abilities, then we need one another. Each of us has a role to play within a community of God's people, working to put the Bible into practice and carry its mission forward into the world.

As the triune Father-Son-Spirit, God is relational in his very nature. He created man and knew that it was not good for him to be alone. The crux of his rescue plan revealed to Abraham in Genesis was not that he would work through empowered individuals but through a family-turned-nation. Jesus poured his Spirit out into his community of followers so that they might go forth into other communities and preach the gospel.

Individualism has fooled us into believing we can walk this road alone, but the enduring evidence throughout the Bible is that we were made for one another. Much like the Communion table,

Scripture is meant to be something we gather around and dine on together. So gather a group of friends (or better yet, a group of folks from different parts of town) and start a Bible book club. Feast on the Bible together, experiencing the joys and challenges of a shared table.

Discover the Bible's World

*The Bible for Christians is not just the Word of God.
Rather, it is the Word of God spoken through people in history.*
KENNETH BAILEY

AS YOU READ BIG and immerse yourself in whole books of the Bible, it won't be long before you notice that God's *strange new world*, mentioned in chapter 4, originated in the middle of a strange old world. Our tendency to pick out easily applicable Verse McNuggets has shielded us from the fact that when we read the Bible, we are reading an anthology of literature from long ago and far away. But now we're out of excuses. It's time to confront and wrestle with the Bible's foreignness.

Long before the words of Scripture were ever printed in English, they were penned in Hebrew and Greek. Genesis 1:1 looked something like this:

בראשית ברא אלהים את השמים ואת הארץ

And John 3:16 looked something like this:

ΟΥΤΩΣΓΑΡΗΓΑΠΗΣΕΝΟΘΕΟΣΤΟΝΚΟΣΜΟΝΩ
ΣΤΕΤΟΝΥΙΟΝΤΟΝΜΟΝΟΓΕΝΗΕΔΩΚΕΝΙΝΑΠΑΣ
ΟΠΙΣΤΕΥΩΝΕΙΣΑΥΤΟΝΜΗΑΠΟΛΗΤΑΙΑΛΛΕΧΗΖ
ΩΗΝΑΙΩΝΙΟΝ

Bible translators have given us an immeasurable gift by rendering God's written Word into languages we can understand, but language itself is only the tip of the iceberg. Language is a product of culture, and culture is made up of the multitudes of norms and values that are assumed and unspoken. Hovering just beneath the Bible's words is the Bible's world, and most of us know very little about it.

Comedian Brian Regan tells a great joke about his first night at college in Ohio. He's in his dorm room with his new roommate, who is from New Jersey, when his roommate pipes up, "Ey, you wanna go halves on a pie?" Regan squints and looks around. "You . . . want to get a pie? Now?" Having grown up in Miami, Florida, Regan had never heard of a pizza referred to as a pie.

"I wanted to be open-minded, you know—it's my first day at college. So I'm like, 'Yeah, okay. Let's get a pie.' So we got half pepperoni, half pumpkin."[1]

Regan was the same age as his roommate, was from the same time period and same country, and spoke the same language, but their slightly different cultural backgrounds still caused his roommate's invitation to get lost in translation. Our Bible was compiled millennia ago and half a world away. The distance between our world and theirs is much greater than that between Miami and New Jersey.

I think most people understand that God inspired real people in real historical settings to compose the literature we call Scripture. The problem is that we don't really know what to do with this fact. How much time, effort, and energy do we have to put into digging beneath the surface to understand the Bible in its ancient and foreign context? Can God still speak to us through the "plain meaning" of the words on the page, or do we need to become Greek and Hebrew experts, parsing a verse at a time, to have any hope of understanding the Scriptures? The path before us seems to diverge into either academia or ignorance.

Don't worry, because there is a middle way. There's a way for the average Christian to continually read big and read whole books with a commitment to ongoing learning about the world of the Bible. My knowledge of Greek ends somewhere between *gyro* and *tzatziki,* but I have fostered a curiosity about the Bible's ancient Near Eastern context. As I've begun to learn more about what's happening behind the scenes and below the surface, I have discovered richness and meaning I never expected. And that's what this chapter is about.

Alas, there's no way to do proper justice to everything under the umbrella of "biblical context" in one measly chapter, so you can think of this chapter as my attempt to crack open the door to the Louvre to give you a peek inside. My goal here is to show you that there's a lifetime's worth of exploration and discovery between Genesis and Revelation.

The Bible is like ogres, in that ogres are like onions. And onions have layers. (If you haven't seen the movie *Shrek,* I can't help you.) If you were to ask a scholar, they might tell you that context in the Bible has six different layers: historical/cultural, literary, narrative, rhetorical, social, and linguistic.[2] In this chapter we're only going to look at two types: historical/cultural and literary.

Thankfully, scholars have done the hard work of diving into the Bible's world and publishing their findings in very accessible resources for regular folks like you and me, so at the end of this chapter you'll find a list of resources you can check out to start your own exploration into the Bible's context.

Historical/Cultural Context

Historical/cultural context is what you probably think of when you hear the word *context*. What was the world like when the books of the Bible were recorded? What was happening behind the scenes of the text itself? What assumptions were present in people's thinking, and what kinds of behavior were normal in their societies?

"In a culture, the most important things usually go without being said," say Randolph Richards and Richard James.[3] There are many parts of the Bible the original recipients could receive without any explanation, so the Bible doesn't explain them. This creates gaps between their world and ours. And when gaps form, two things can happen:

1. *Substitution.* We don't read the Bible as neutral observers. We bring our own cultural values and assumptions to our reading, so we're prone to automatically and subconsciously substitute our values and norms for theirs. We assume that a character was motivated to act a certain way because of XYZ when really they acted because of ABC. This can lead to misinterpretation and misapplication.

2. *Confusion.* Oftentimes, we will come across a scenario for which we don't have a cultural substitute, so the gap between our worlds remains. We're left confused and sometimes disturbed by what a character says or does because we can't fathom what would prompt them to do it.

Once we begin to understand the historical situations, cultural values, and implicit assumptions present in the Bible's world, the gaps begin to close. The characters start to feel human, and their motivations, while still admittedly unfamiliar to our sensibilities, are no longer unfathomable. Again, this section could occupy thousands of pages, but here is a glimpse at just a few important historical and cultural realities to keep in mind while you read.

Empire

Since the Bible takes place in the midst of real history, real historical power structures play an important role in its story. The vast majority of the Bible is written from the perspective of people on the bottom, not the top, of the power structure. Early on, we see Egypt as a superpower that enslaves the Hebrew people for generations. God liberates them and leads them into their own land, where Israel grows into a powerful nation under King David. Tragically, their idolatry and infidelity to God bring their own destruction. The nation splits in two and is taken into captivity by the Assyrian Empire (in the North) and then the Babylonian Empire (in the South).

By the time of the New Testament, it's the Roman Empire that has its foot on the neck of God's people. This is the world Jesus is born into: a nation longing for a Messiah to free them from oppression and restore them to the glory days of King David—days of power, prosperity, independence, and intimacy with God. Each of the prevailing Jewish sects of the day—the Pharisees, Sadducees, Essenes, and Zealots—have their own ideas about what the people must do to restore God's favor, in the hope that he will free them from Rome's iron grip.

Jesus comes and offers a redefinition of power as he preaches an alternative kingdom. This isn't a campaign to elevate Israel back to its former national glory. Rome isn't the real problem, and neither were the empires that oppressed God's people before. God has indeed come on a rescue mission, but he's there to rescue the world from the dark forces and evil powers undergirding every empire and at work within every human heart.

He is hung naked on a Roman cross, a tool of the empire used to strike terror and shame into their subjects. This is the opposite of a King David victory, yet it is an ironic coronation ceremony. The soldiers of the empire crown Jesus with thorns and anoint him with spit, then raise him up on a throne of wood and nails. This is how the kingdom of God is established on earth; it is a kingdom founded on love, which no empire can conquer.

Patriarchy

After Adam and Eve's sin in the Garden of Eden, the rest of the Bible's story is steeped in cultures that operate with an ingrained gender hierarchy, where men are empowered and women are not, where sons are prized and daughters don't count. A woman's value is derived from the men she is associated with: who her father is, who her husband is, and who her sons are. The first-century Jewish historian Josephus wrote, "The woman . . . is in all things inferior to the man."[4] Rabbinical Jewish leaders would recite this prayer daily: "Praise be to God that he has not created me a Gentile! Praise be to God that he has not created me a woman! Praise be to God that he has not created me an ignoramus!"[5]

In Jewish, Greek, and Roman cultures, wives were often treated more as property than as people. A Roman husband had legal ownership of his wife and all her possessions. For the most part, Greek women were not allowed to speak in public. Jewish law allowed a husband to divorce a dissatisfactory wife, but wives did not have the same right.

This patriarchal culture sets the table for the Bible to interject with some radical stories of female agency and power. Only 10 percent of the Bible's characters are women, yet many of them have highly consequential roles in the story. The Old Testament[6] tells of Miriam, the sister of Moses and Aaron, who played a major part in bringing Israel out of Egypt. In the book of Judges, Deborah served as a prophet, judge, and military leader. The books of Esther and Ruth tell extended stories of women who stood up in bravery and creativity to continue moving God's purposes forward.

Then Jesus arrives on the scene and turns everything on its head. "When we read what Jesus did with regard to women, it should be recognized as countercultural, highly shocking, and extremely challenging to the religious leaders of his day," says Dan Kimball.[7] He freely converses publicly with women, including women of bad reputation. He includes women in his traveling group and even treats them as his students, both things that were viewed as completely scandalous.

Perhaps most significantly, the Bible tells us that women were the first witnesses to the Resurrection, the first people entrusted with the gospel message. Traditionally, this would have been the most ridiculous way to establish the credibility of the Good News—according to Jewish law, women were not allowed to bear legal witness—but Jesus overturns the patriarchal norms with a message of empowerment and status for women. Carolyn Custis James says, "Patriarchy is . . . 'the fallen cultural backdrop' that sets off in the strongest relief the radical nature and potency of the Bible's gospel message."[8]

Community Orientation

Perhaps the biggest mindset shift Westerners have to make when reading the Bible is from our native individualism to a culture of community orientation. Individualistic ideals like personal identity, self-expression, independence, and self-reliance are baked into our American value system. Disney movies have taught us to "follow your heart" and "believe in yourself" as we chase after our dreams. The rights to personal liberties and freedom of expression appear throughout our founding documents.

The merits and pitfalls of these values are up for debate, but one thing is clear for our purposes: They don't line up with the values and assumptions present in the Bible. The ancient Near East was a highly communal society, which means the group came first. Identity was based not in the individual person but in the family, tribe, region, or nation a person came from: "Jesus of Nazareth"; "Saul of Tarsus"; "John, son of Zebedee"; "Simon the Zealot."

During the twentieth century, a social psychologist named Geert Hofstede surveyed people from across fifty-three nations and found that the most individualistic countries in the world were the United States, Australia, and Great Britain. Not only that, but their individualism scores were *more than double* the global norm.[9]

There's no way for us to get rid of our individualism, but we do need to be aware of it and try to read with a more communal perspective. It's good to pay attention to a character's personal story, but we should also try to notice what is happening within the *relationships* in the story. Read carefully and try to figure out when *you* would be more accurately read as *y'all*. Ask questions about the roles tribes, nations, and families may have played in a given scenario.

To help illustrate this, we can take a quick look at one way Jesus shook things up in a communal society. In cultures where personal identity is drawn from the surrounding community, one's family is at the very heart of it all. So when Jesus shows up and begins asking questions like *Who is my mother, and who are my brothers?* he is challenging the very foundation of their society.

"Pointing to his disciples, he said, 'Here are my mother and my brothers. For whoever does the will of my Father in heaven is my brother and sister and mother.'"[10]

By redefining familial boundaries, Jesus reorients his audience's strongest bond and deepest identity marker. This new family of God, founded in Christ, welcomes people from every nation, tribe, and tongue. It eliminates any preexisting identity markers that would otherwise draw boundaries between us. As Dominique DuBois Gilliard puts it: "Everything in this world teaches us that blood is thicker than water. . . . The Scriptures tell us that the baptismal waters are thicker than our ancestral blood."[11]

Literary Context

If historical/cultural context is about understanding the assumed realities of a culture and society, literary context focuses on the unspoken rules necessary to engage properly with different genres of literature.

This might sound like something out of high school English class, but it's actually a mental process we engage in every day. Without thinking about it, we automatically understand the differences between a biography and a newspaper op-ed or between a poem and a legal contract. We know that different genres need to be read differently.

We've established in previous chapters that the Bible is a library of literature and that using a reader's Bible will help us visually perceive the type of literature we're reading. But there are inconspicuous differences between ancient letters and the letters we receive in our mailbox today. The structure of Hebrew poetry plays an important role in its meaning. Ancient narratives, history, and biographies have different priorities than our modern versions. And, of course, there are ancient genres that are totally unfamiliar to us, like wisdom literature and apocalypse.

Understanding the conventions of the Bible's literature is key to understanding what the author is trying to communicate. We don't have time to look at all the different genres, but here is a glimpse beneath the surface of a few.

Ancient Letters

About one-third of the Bible's books are letters. Typically written by leaders to give authoritative teaching to a community when they weren't physically present, letters follow a three-part structure.

In the opening, the writer states their name and who they're writing to and offers a thanksgiving for their recipients. The body of the letter deals with the purpose at hand, and the closing includes personal greetings, prayer requests, and a blessing for the recipients.

With this in mind, we can now notice that Paul's letter to the Galatians conspicuously neglects the traditional thanksgiving in the opening. He begins 1 Corinthians with "I always thank my God for you and for the gracious gifts he has given you, now that you belong to Christ Jesus."[12] Philippians starts with "Every time I think of you, I give thanks to my God."[13]

Galatians? Nada. The church would have been waiting for a thanksgiving similar to the ones given to the Corinthians and the Philippians, so they were likely caught off guard when Paul jumped right in with a rebuke: "I am shocked that you are turning away so soon from God, who called you to himself through the loving mercy of Christ. You are following a different way that pretends to be the Good News."[14] He's ticked, and he wants them to know it.

Apocalypse

Growing up, the word *apocalypse* conjured up mental pictures of fire, crumbled buildings, and mushroom clouds. Many of us have seen movies involving a zombie apocalypse, and some especially creative science fiction writers have even dreamed up a scenario called the Alpacalypse, wherein hordes of the fluffy, long-necked creatures violently take over the world. Seriously, look it up.

It's understandable that many modern readers bring this popular end-of-the-world definition into their reading of the apocalyptic literature found throughout the Bible, most notably in

Daniel and Revelation. But apocalypse was a genre utilized by the biblical authors on multiple occasions, and a better definition is "unveiling."

In apocalyptic literature, a heavenly visitor, such as an angel, comes to reveal supernatural realities to a human recipient. Using rich imagery and coded language (i.e., really weird stuff), this special revelation allows the human author to see present and future events from a divine perspective.

Apocalypse is complicated, but thinking of it as a recipe for the end times will cause you to misread it. We are not dealing with concrete descriptions but rather analogies and metaphors that reveal the spiritual magnitude of the situations they portray. While there are certainly allusions to future events, a lot of the symbols in the Bible's apocalyptic literature focus on unveiling the deeper realities of the first recipients' current events. Many of the symbols in Revelation, for example, illustrate the persecution first-century Christians were enduring from the tyrannical, beastly Roman emperor Domitian.

Interpreting apocalyptic literature will never be straightforward or easy, but it helps to remember that we're reading recordings of visions given to people in specific historical circumstances. For example, Revelation uses the illustration of a woman sitting upon a beast with seven heads, which the angel explains, "represent the seven hills where the woman rules."[15] First-century Christians would have recognized the imagery as referring to Rome, a city built upon seven hills.

So, if the Bible's apocalyptic literature was primarily meant to pull back the curtain for ancient audiences in specific circumstances, is there any reason for us to read it? Absolutely. In the midst of all the monsters and blood, apocalypse reminds us of the unseen spiritual realm where God is continually working. It gives us "a heavenly perspective on our earthly circumstances so that every generation of God's people can be challenged, comforted, and given hope for the future."[16]

Wisdom Literature

Wisdom literature is another one of the Bible's genres that didn't quite make it into our modern world. We may have folksy American proverbs like *The early bird gets the worm* and *Don't count your chickens before they hatch*, and there are the pithy sayings inside our Chinese fortune cookies, but we don't have much literature that helps us meditate on the complexities of living well in the world.

What kind of world did God make? How can we live in tune with his created order? What is the good life, and how do we get it? These are the profound questions at the heart of the Old Testament's wisdom literature: Job, Psalms, Proverbs, Ecclesiastes, and the Song of Songs. We'll focus on Proverbs, Ecclesiastes, and Job.

The book of Proverbs begins by setting the stage. It casts wisdom as a woman calling out in the streets, inviting people to come and listen to her teaching:

> How long will you who are simple love your simple ways?
>> How long will mockers delight in mockery
>> and fools hate knowledge?
> Repent at my rebuke!
>> Then I will pour out my thoughts to you,
>> I will make known to you my teachings.[17]

As we continue reading, we get the sense that wisdom is woven into the very fabric of God's created world. When people live wisely, they move with the grain of how God intended things to be, and life will go well for them. When they live as fools, they go against the grain and away from the good life God designed. Proverbs contains hundreds of punchy, practical sayings that give guidance for living in the fear of the Lord, which is the path to an abundant life of health and prosperity.

Unfortunately, modern readers who are unfamiliar with the ancient wisdom genre will often mistake proverbs for promises. Many parents have been shocked and deeply distressed that, after years of hard work to "train up a child in the way he should go,"[18] the child indeed departs from it. In real life, the wicked frequently prosper while the righteous suffer. Proverbs give us wisdom about the way life should generally work, but they are not guarantees. Life, as we will see, is much more complicated than that.

"Meaningless!" Ecclesiastes shouts from the couch, three hours into its binge-watch of *The Price Is Right*. "Everything is meaningless."[19]

Ecclesiastes knows all about the straightforward sayings of Proverbs, but it's here to offer a different perspective on the human experience: Life is fleeting. Life is inconsistent. Life is complex. We can pursue the wisdom offered by Proverbs and sometimes things will go well for us, but things can just as often go poorly. For Ecclesiastes, life is a roulette table. Or, perhaps, a Plinko board.

So what does Ecclesiastes suggest? Enjoy the little things. Pursue the wisdom offered by Proverbs, but don't necessarily expect success and prosperity to follow. Life is too confusing and too mysterious to grab hold of and master. We don't have ultimate control over our lives, but rather than filling ourselves with existential dread, we can choose to relish the simple gifts of a good meal and time with a friend.

Even more significantly, Ecclesiastes assures us that God is still actively working in ways we can't discern. One day he will clear away the smoke that obscures the realities of life and bring our actions to light. Like Proverbs, Ecclesiastes ends with this advice: "Fear God and keep his commandments, for this is the duty of all mankind."[20]

The book of Job takes the conversation a step further. Job is exactly the kind of man Proverbs envisions: righteous, wise, full of integrity and reverence for God. And in the beginning of the book, his life displays the results that Proverbs describes. He is healthy and wealthy, with a big, beautiful family.

Then disaster arrives. All Job's livestock is either killed or stolen, all his children die, and he's struck with a skin disease that covers him in boils. The majority of the book of Job contains poetic dialogue between Job and his friends about what he must have done to deserve such suffering.

Job contains deep explorations into God's goodness and the justice he has woven into the world. What happens when life moves beyond the straightforwardness of Proverbs, past the randomness of Ecclesiastes, and into what seems like overt injustice for Job?

Toward the end of the book, Job challenges God to account for his actions. God does come and speak, but he doesn't explain himself. Instead, he declares that he doesn't have to. He takes Job on a tour of creation from the depths of the seas up into the stars, showing that Job knows nothing about the immense intricacies and complexities of God's rule. "Do you still want to argue with the Almighty? You are God's critic, but do you have the answers?"[21] Job is flattened. "I take back everything I said, and I sit in dust and ashes to show my repentance."[22]

Job shows us that no easy comfort or blame will be found in simplistic formulas about God. God alone sees all things, and our lives are to be lived in faith, trusting in him to set all things right.

So how can we read wisdom literature well? First off, this is a genre where it helps to slow down a bit. In chapter 4, I argued for picking up the pace to get a landscape view of books, but reading ten pages of Proverbs in one sitting will leave your head spinning. The wisdom contained in these books is worth marinating in, so take smaller bites and chew on them. Meditate, reflect, and pray for wisdom.

Second, it's helpful to read these three books in conversation with one another. They each have a different perspective on the good life, and there is tension between their ideas. But like three notes coming together to form a chord, they join to make one sound: Trust in the Lord. All wisdom is rooted in submission to the Creator. Trust in his goodness through the prosperity, chaos, and suffering that we will encounter in this life under the sun.

Pursuing Understanding

At this point, it may be worth a check-in. With all this talk about history and culture and literature, you might be unsure whether the Bible can even speak to us at all if we haven't done the proper work to understand its various layers of context. You might also be wondering if, after all we've been through, I've made a U-turn back toward study Bibles and Bible study. Here's what I think.

First off, I absolutely believe that God can speak to us through the Bible despite our lack of understanding. We can approach the text with confidence that the Spirit is present in the midst of our reading, revealing goodness and truth along the way.

But we must also approach the Bible with humility. We need to acknowledge the reality that although the Bible is *for* us, it was not originally written *to* us—that these are ancient, foreign documents full of intricacies that aren't immediately recognizable to our modern eyes. "Anyone can read the Bible and be blessed by that reading, just as anyone can listen to a Bach cantata and be moved," says Dr. Kenneth Bailey. "But at the same time, the trained ear will hear more and be moved on a deeper level by the same music."[23]

Pink Floyd's famous album cover for *The Dark Side of the Moon* shows a white beam of light traveling across a black expanse, hitting a triangular prism, and refracting into a rainbow of colors. While it's not a perfect metaphor (I think a non-contextual reading of the Bible contains more than a thin beam of "light"), reading through the prism of ancient context will help us experience Scripture in full color.

So how do we do that? Do we need to revert back to microscopic Bible study as our primary method of engaging with the Bible? Not at all. Reader's Bibles should remain primary, and reading should remain primary. When we read big rather than in isolated snippets, we automatically pick up on layers of context that we would have otherwise missed.

But after you read big, go back into a book with an investigative eye. Slow down and read critically, asking questions about what might be going on below the surface. Use a study Bible for what it's good for: looking things up and finding extra information.

Grab a commentary from a respected scholar and see what they've uncovered in their studies. Ask your church leadership to begin teaching classes on biblical interpretation and context.

Work some books about the Bible into your reading schedule or some podcasts into your listening lineup. World-class content is more freely and readily available than ever before. Take advantage of the brilliant men and women who have dedicated their lives to helping people understand the ancient world of the Bible. And, of course, involve your community by reading together, asking questions, and drawing from the collective knowledge of the group.

This isn't about getting the Bible all figured out. No matter how contextually we read, Scripture will remain full of mystery, pointing us toward a God beyond our comprehension. This is about cultivating a lifestyle of biblical curiosity and a pursuit of understanding. For several generations, we Christians have prioritized loving God with our hearts, souls, and strength, but in some ways we've struggled to love him with our minds. Seeking a better understanding of the intricate ways he has acted through people and literature and history to move his purposes forward will deepen our love for him and our appreciation for the gospel. It will refine our theology and strengthen our witness. As we'll see in upcoming chapters, it will clarify the Bible's story and our role within it.

Resources for Understanding the Bible in Context

- book introductions in *Immerse: The Reading Bible*
- videos by BibleProject
- *Misreading Scripture with Western Eyes* by E. Randolph Richards and Brandon J. O'Brien

- *Misreading Scripture with Individualist Eyes* by E. Randolph Richards and Richard James
- *How (Not) to Read the Bible* by Dan Kimball
- A Week in the Life series by InterVarsity Press
- *Scripture as Communication* by Jeannine K. Brown
- *Jesus through Middle Eastern Eyes* by Kenneth E. Bailey
- *NIV Cultural Backgrounds Study Bible* edited by John H. Walton and Craig S. Keener
- *IVP Bible Background Commentary: Old Testament* by John H. Walton
- *IVP Bible Background Commentary: New Testament* by Craig S. Keener
- The Lost World series by John H. Walton
- *The New Testament in Its World* by N. T. Wright and Michael F. Bird

PART THREE

story

The Story We Find Ourselves In

*The first responsibility
of a leader is to define reality.*
MAX DE PREE

WE COME NOW TO THE HEART OF THINGS. Everything we've covered so far, from the physical format of our Bibles to our regular habits and practices, has been in service to the bigger questions and concepts we'll be exploring in the final part of this book.

What is the Bible? Like, at a fundamental level? What is it actually *for*? For most people, these foundational questions are never really explored in any sort of meaningful or comprehensive way. We know that, as good Christians, we're supposed to read the Bible, but many of us were never really taught *why*.

And so each of us is left to form (or inherit) our own default assumptions, conscious or unconscious, about what the Bible is and what role it's supposed to play in our lives. To borrow a more technical word from the scientific community, we create our own

Bible *paradigms*, defined as "framework[s] containing . . . basic assumptions, ways of thinking, and methodology."[1] These paradigms deeply shape our expectations for the Bible, dictating why and how we engage with it.

Some people operate with the paradigm that the Bible is primarily a reminder of God's love, so they go to it for reassurance and encouragement to help them cope with the difficulties of life. For others, it's a sourcebook of doctrine and truth that we must learn, adhere to, and defend. Still others understand it as an instruction manual for right living. Read it, do what it says, and you'll come out all right.

The problem with these characterizations is not necessarily that they're incorrect but that they're incomplete. As we explored in chapter 4, subjecting the Bible to our agendas will invariably force us into small and selective readings. If I believe that the Bible exists primarily for my encouragement, then I have to admit that I'm not really sure what to do with the vast majority of Scripture, which doesn't fit that model. The same goes if my expectation is for doctrine, ethics, rules, commands, and so on.

What kind of paradigm can support the weight of all these various expectations? What model can handle the whole Bible?

The truth is, all the Bible's encouragement, correction, doctrine, commands, instructions, and wisdom live within the tent of its "immense, sprawling, capacious narrative."[2] At its core, the Bible is a *story*.

Now, you've probably heard that term used to describe the Bible, and you're not alone if you feel a little bit skeptical about it. After all, *story* can mean lots of different things. Fairy tales are stories spun up from active imaginations. Politicians and salespeople distort the truth to fit the stories they tell in order to sell something or advance an agenda. Stories are oftentimes squishy, subjective, and open to interpretation. If we're going to base our lives on the Bible, we're going to need something more reliable than a story.

I get it. But we don't need to be suspicious of story. Story is how we understand who we are.

Historians, psychologists, sociologists, and anthropologists have all studied the role of narrative within the human experience and nearly unanimously affirm that stories are the vehicle through which humans understand the world and assign meaning to life.

"Consciousness begins when brains acquire the power, the simple power I must add, of telling a story,"[3] writes neuroscientist Antonio Damasio. Developmental psychologists believe that children as young as one year old begin perceiving an "autobiographical self," seeing themselves as the narrator of their experiences. Our internal narrative grows in complexity and detail as we get older. When we reach our adolescent and young-adult years, we begin to construct a life story, or what psychologists call *narrative identity*: where we came from, what we've experienced, the challenges in our past and present, and the future we are striving toward. Our conceptions of ourselves are built upon our story.[4]

Think about a time when you met a new acquaintance for coffee or went out to dinner on a first date. The person you were meeting could have given you a one-page fact sheet of bullet points about themselves—where they were born, how many siblings they had, where they went to school, and so on—but that would have hardly been satisfying. When we meet somebody new, we get to know them by learning their story and sharing ours.

Or consider the classic detective movie. The investigator is back at the station, leaning against a desk, studying a corkboard pinned with mug shots, receipts, flight itineraries, and bank documents. The data is right in front of her, but how is it all related? In order to begin making sense of it all, she needs the red string zig zagged across the board, connecting the dots. Information acquires meaning when it's linked together by the red string of narrative.

Because God created us as story-driven creatures, story seeps into nearly every element of our lives. We have our personal stories, but we also have shared community stories with our families, nations, ethnicities, and workplaces. Nearly everything we encounter in life, from insurance ads to sports championships to presidential elections, can be viewed and understood through the lens of story.

Finally, all these stories take place within a big story, also known as a metanarrative. Metanarratives help us make sense of our lives within the comprehensive story of the whole world—past, present, and future. "I cannot answer the question, 'What ought I to do?'" said the philosopher Alasdair MacIntyre, "unless I first answer the question, 'Of which story am I a part?'"[5]

Many of us have inherited a paradigm of the Bible as a collection of unconnected dots—of stories and verses and propositions pinned to a corkboard without any red string attached. But the Bible's bold claim, the claim that we must be audacious enough to believe if the Bible is going to accomplish its mission in our lives, is that it contains the ultimate metanarrative: *the true story of the whole world.*

"In the beginning, God created the heavens and the earth."[6] By the end of the first sentence, the stage is set, and we've met the protagonist. This is a story about the infinite, eternal Creator and his creation. Its scope is not merely private and spiritual but cosmic and all-encompassing.

From there, we're introduced to humans, the other primary actors in the drama, whose choices will play a crucial role in influencing the story's direction. God reveals that he doesn't intend to rule as a distant colonizer but rather that he's designed his world so that he can live alongside his image bearers in perfect harmony. Humans are infused with a purpose—a vocation to cultivate and tend to the creation, co-ruling as stewards of the cosmic kingdom. Their ability to fulfill this vocation depends entirely on their unique relationship with the Creator.

So when they reject their vocation and rebel against the one who made them, they bring catastrophe upon the entire created order.

Very quickly, the story is off and running. We soon find out that the family of Abraham, the ancient nation of Israel, figures prominently into God's rescue plan. Their story will be a microcosm of the human story. The Old Testament makes up a full three-fourths of the Bible and contains the crucial rising action of the Creator's work to fix what has gone horribly wrong in his creation. We'll explore this more in the next chapter.

Jesus at the Center of the Story

The odd thing about the Bible's story (well, one of the odd things) is that most people get introduced to it via its climax—that is, most people don't start in Genesis and read straight through, wondering how the story is going to turn out. The gateway into faith and into the Scriptures is Christ on the cross. Our journey into the Bible doesn't usually start with "In the beginning" but rather "It is finished."[7]

Somehow, this scandalous and unsettling image draws us in. The story of Jesus' sacrifice and victory and rescue opens a Pandora's box of questions: *Who is this man? Why did he have to die? Victory over what? Rescue from what?* And this is exactly the right place to start.

In 1543, a Polish astronomer named Nicolaus Copernicus published *On the Revolutions of the Heavenly Spheres*, a book containing the theory of the heliocentric model of the universe. Copernicus believed that the Sun lay at the center of the cosmos, serving as the point around which all the universe's planets and other celestial bodies revolved. His theory refuted the widely held geocentric model that the Earth was at the center.

One of the Christian church's oldest and most central reading practices is the *Christocentric* reading of Scripture—that is, reading the entirety of the Bible's story in the Old and New Testaments as revolving around Jesus. He is the center, the focal point, of all of the Bible. "The Old Testament points forward to him; the New Testament points back to him," writes Stuart Murray.[8] We read the entire canon of Scripture, Old and New Testaments, in order to continually add more lines of detail and brushstrokes of color to the person of Jesus. At the same time, somewhat paradoxically, by understanding Jesus better we gain more clarity when interpreting the rest of the Bible, which then circles back to a better understanding of Jesus. Let me explain.

First off, we must accept that Jesus was born into the long and winding story of the Scriptures that started before he entered the world as a flesh-and-blood man. All four of the Gospels begin by referencing the Old Testament: Matthew ties Jesus to the family line of David and Abraham; Mark quotes from the prophet Isaiah; John connects Jesus all the way back to the Creation story in Genesis.

Luke begins his Gospel with a much more investigative preface but quickly connects Elizabeth, John the Baptist's mother, to Aaron, the brother of Moses. The angel Gabriel promises Zechariah that his son, John, will "bring back many of the people of Israel to the Lord their God. And he will go on before the Lord, in the spirit and power of Elijah, to turn the hearts of the parents to their children and the disobedient to the wisdom of the righteous—to make ready a people prepared for the Lord."[9]

Throughout the Gospels, we are confronted by Jesus' unmistakable Jewishness. He lives in Jewish communities, participates in Jewish traditions and festivals, teaches in Jewish synagogues, and is enmeshed in Jewish debates. His language is packed with quotes from the Psalms, the Torah, and the Prophets.

Even the word *Messiah* (and its Greek equivalent, *Christ*) has become such a part of our Christian vocabulary that we often forget it was a title. The Messiah was Israel's Anointed One, their long-awaited rescuer. It was a role pregnant with expectations of liberation and victory. When Jesus is born, the shepherds of the field and Simeon and Anna at the Jerusalem Temple all jump for joy. The one they have been waiting for is, at long last, here.

"Those who read the Bible with Christ at the center understand Jesus as reenacting, as well as completing, Israel's history," writes New Testament scholar Dennis Edwards.[10] Jesus constantly and intentionally acts in ways that echo the story of Israel told in the Old Testament, except he succeeds where they failed.

We must remember that Jesus didn't drop out of heaven and start a new story. When we amputate him from the Israel story he was born into, when we trade the first-century Jewish Jesus for a generic Jesus, we won't get a fully formed picture of who he is. "The Bible is the God-given means through which we know who Jesus is," says N. T. Wright. "Take the Bible away, diminish it or water it down, and you are free to invent a Jesus just a little bit different from the Jesus who is hidden in the Old Testament and revealed in the New."[11]

It is simply not an option to write off the Old Testament and focus on Jesus. If he is the climax and turning point of the story that has come before, it is our responsibility to continually familiarize ourselves with that story. We must read all of the Bible, even the boring, strange, confusing, and hard-to-read parts, because they all contribute to our understanding of Jesus.

"Do not think that I have come to abolish the Law or the Prophets," he says during the Sermon on the Mount. "I have not come to abolish them but to fulfill them."[12]

How exactly does he fulfill them, though? A surface-level reading of the Law and Prophets can give us the impression that Jesus stepped onto the set of the wrong production. This is the second half of the puzzle of how to read the story well.

In 1999, blue-eyed, baby-faced actor Haley Joel Osment effectively creeped out much of the Western world when he whispered four little words: "I see dead people."

M. Night Shyamalan's psychological thriller *The Sixth Sense* introduced us to ten-year-old Cole Sear, a severely troubled young boy who can see and interact with the spirits of dead people. He gets paired up with child psychologist Dr. Malcolm Crowe (played by Bruce Willis), and the movie chronicles their relationship as Crowe tries to figure out how to free young Cole from the disturbing visions. Eventually Crowe overcomes his skepticism about Cole's condition and suggests that instead of being afraid of the spirits, Cole should learn to help them. His idea ends up being the solution to Cole's terror and paranoia, and Cole transforms into a normal, happy kid—the kind of kid he's always wanted to be.

As the movie is coming to a close and loose ends are being tied up, Shyamalan hits the audience with an enormous sucker punch: Dr. Crowe realizes that *he is dead*.

The tectonic plot twist forces you to rethink everything about the movie you just watched. It was a good story before, but realizing that Crowe has been interacting with Cole as one of the dead spirits casts *everything* in a different light. When you go back and rewatch it, you catch little hints and oddities that you didn't notice before but that now make perfect sense, given that Crowe is actually a ghost. The entire story gets turned on its head because of one stunning revelation.

This is kind of like what Jesus does to the Bible's story. He is not simply the climax and fulfillment of Israel's story but also the shocking twist.

As he preaches and teaches around Galilee, Judea, and Samaria, his disciples and closest friends constantly struggle to see how he fits into their understanding of the Jewish narrative. The religious leaders eventually have him killed because they can't reconcile him with their paradigm of how God is supposed to act in the world.

Then, on a dusty road to Emmaus, the risen Jesus meets two of his followers who, despite their lack of understanding, that "had hoped that he was the one who was going to redeem Israel."[13]

"How foolish you are, and how slow to believe all that the prophets have spoken! Did not the Messiah have to suffer these things and then enter his glory?" he asks. Luke adds, "And beginning with Moses and all the Prophets, he explained to them what was said in all the Scriptures concerning himself."[14]

The twist in the story, hidden all along, is that Jesus is the yes to all God's promises to Abraham. His way of being the Messiah was the way it always had to be. He's also the truly human one, the kind of human Adam was supposed to be, living in complete obedience and harmony with the Father. His life, death, and resurrection don't only fulfill Israel's story; they also set the story of humanity back on track.

This turning point forced any first-century Jew to decide if they would reframe and recalibrate everything in light of Jesus. Doing so would require them to shift their entire understanding of their Scriptures, the mission of God, and the trajectory of the world. They would have to put Jesus in the center as the interpretive key for the entire story.

The conversion of Saul of Tarsus gives us a dramatic example of the kind of reorientation a God-fearing Jew would go through in order to believe and profess the gospel of Messiah Jesus. A zealous Pharisee, Saul is glad to kill Christians who worship this so-called Savior. He is living the Israel story, and thus the human story, a certain way. The blinding light of Jesus (literally and symbolically) on the road to Damascus forces him to rethink everything he thinks he knows, and he is transformed into Paul, the apostle to the Gentiles.

Much of the rest of the New Testament (in which Paul plays a huge part) is about unpacking all the ways Jesus is the fulfillment of Israel's Scriptures and the turning point of world history. The written Word has to be reexamined in light of the living Word. "The apostles did not arrive at the conclusion that Jesus is Lord from a dispassionate, objective reading of the Old Testament," writes progressive Old Testament scholar Peter Enns. "Rather, they began with what they knew to be true—the historical death and resurrection of the Son of God—and on the basis of that fact reread their Scripture in a fresh way."[15]

For our Bible reading, this means the best and most authentic way to read the story is to read all of it through the Jesus lens. Just like Dr. Crowe's status in *The Sixth Sense*, Jesus is the deeper reality, hidden at first but now revealed. We can read the Bible and take its teaching at face value, but it must always be examined in light of Jesus, the truest and fullest revelation of God.

For instance, Dr. Michael Bird comments that we can read the story of King David's adultery with Bathsheba and come away with true and valuable lessons about lust, violence, and exploitation. But now, in light of Jesus, we can also see David's place within the larger story. We can see that in the grand scheme of God's rescue, Israel's greatest king fell far short of God's standards. Despite being called a man after God's own heart, David is merely a broken and imperfect foreshadowing, a signpost pointing toward the Son of David, the true and perfect representation of God, the world's true King.[16]

To summarize, our task today is the same as the first Christians two millennia ago: to become fluent in the whole story of Scripture, inside and out, so we can see how it's all about Jesus. It's easy to get frustrated and flabbergasted by the boring, strange, and confusing parts of the Bible, to throw up our hands and say, "Just give me Jesus!" But the person of Jesus and the story of Scripture are inseparable; isolating them from each other will cause both to become shrunken and distorted.

Reading the story with Jesus at the center means moving back and forth between the Gospels and the rest of the Bible, using each to clarify and reinforce the other. Doing this is only possible through the Holy Spirit, who opens our eyes to see how God has been relentlessly steering the biblical narrative back toward his mission of salvation and redemption through Jesus.

We read big, and we read whole books; we read and discuss in community; and we strive to better understand the layers of ancient context. We do all this *so that* we can become more fluent in the vast and multifaceted story of the Bible, throughout which Christ is present in every branch and tendril.

"Scripture is more than information revealed for our knowledge so that, in knowing more, we will be more," says Scot McKnight. "In fact, Scripture is God's word for God's people so that in hearing this word in communion with others we learn how to walk in this world in the way of Jesus."[17]

Choosing Our Story

So here's the thing about metanarratives: We can only have one. That is, we only have room in our hearts for one core story—one fundamental operating framework for the world, who we are, why we're here, and where things are going. We may find ways to fit elements of other narratives alongside or underneath our core story, but there can only be one story at the center of our hearts. And the competition is fierce.

Our world is a marketplace of stories all vying for our attention, affection, and allegiance: consumerism, nationalism, free-market capitalism, communism, atheism, modernism, postmodernism, partisan politics, the American dream. The list goes on.

Here in America, the marketplace of stories is perhaps bigger and more varied than ever before. Our increasingly diverse and pluralistic society combined with the splintering of media brought on by cable TV, the internet, and social media means a torrent of various stories is coming at us from all angles all the time. We're endlessly bombarded with proposed answers to the five basic questions that, according to theologian N. T. Wright, make up a worldview:

1. Who are we?
2. Where are we?
3. What is wrong?
4. How is this to be put right?
5. What time is it? (In other words, Where are we in the story?)[18]

Worldviews are often unstated and taken for granted, which makes them even more powerful. Introduced via our habits and the stories we passively absorb, they creep in through the back door of our consciousness, silently shaping how we see the world. "A worldview is not what you look *at* but what you look *through*."[19]

In his book *You Are What You Love*, James K. A. Smith examines the worldview produced by just one of the pervading stories that shapes Western society: consumerism. Consumerism has no holy scriptures and no ordained priests, but the power of its narrative permeates nearly every moment of our lives. The story consumerism tells us about the world and about what it means to be human radically orients our desires toward certain goals and fills our imaginations with definitions of the good life.

Smith argues that we aren't discipled into the story of consumerism through conscious, rational decisions but through the habits and practices we're involved in every day. "I don't *think* my way into consumerism. Rather, I'm covertly conscripted into a way of life because I have been *formed* by cultural practices that are nothing less than secular liturgies. . . . 'Liturgy,' as I'm using the word, is a shorthand term for those rituals that are loaded with an ultimate Story about who we are and what we're for. They carry within them a kind of ultimate orientation."[20]

So, every time we watch a YouTube review for the latest tech gadget, every time we flick through Instagram and see that one influencer on yet another trip to the Caribbean, every time we come across a beer commercial featuring a group of friends laughing on a boat, we're engaging in secular liturgies that *do something* to us. Every advertisement preaches a sermon about the good life, about happiness and fulfillment and pleasure, along with the silent accusation that *this isn't you, is it? But maybe it could be, if you just bought that thing.*

It's a simple story, but it's one that disciples us into a kingdom that seeks to rival the kingdom of Christ. The kingdom of consumerism is built on alternative answers to the five questions listed above, directing our hearts to worship alternative gods. And it is merely one among the multitudes of stories we're exposed to.

If we're never taught that the Bible contains the true story of the whole world, centered on the person of Jesus Christ, we will inevitably latch onto a story from somewhere else. A minimalized, summarized, and chopped-up version of Scripture can't stand up to the onslaught of narratives offering us enticing explanations of who we are and what we're here for. Without our even realizing it, the alternative stories become our core story, and we pick and choose the parts of the Bible that seem to fit into it. And in many corners of the American church, this is exactly what has happened.

If I had to diagnose the main source of the anemia, divisiveness, and confusion plaguing many Christians in America, it would be that we've lost our story. We've allowed ourselves to be discipled into alternative stories preached by cable news anchors, politicians, corporations, and social media feeds. Old Testament scholar Walter Brueggemann writes that many of us have settled for a "generic U. S. identity that is part patriotism, part consumerism, part violence, and part affluence."[21]

My generation and the generations after us are walking away from the faith because we're being shown a story that is muddy and incoherent at best and hypocritical at worst. We sing about the victory of Jesus on Sunday, then watch as people who claim to follow Christ participate in partisan politics just as feverishly and with just as much vitriol as everyone else. We listen to sermons about God's restoration of all things and then witness many believers who, unable to come to grips with anything but the most romantic version of our nation's history, spit at the feet of those who claim they have been oppressed and mistreated during America's rise to superpower status.[22]

The Bible's grand narrative has been reduced to a bumper-sticker summary of Creation-Fall-Jesus-heaven and sequestered into the "spiritual" corner of our hearts and minds, while we leave the real operation of the world to the stories told by the world. "The question is whether the faith that finds its focus in Jesus is the faith with which we seek to understand the whole of history, or whether we limit this faith to a private world of religion and hand over the public history of the world to other principles of explanation," writes Lesslie Newbigin.[23]

How can we find our way out of this muck and mire? The first step, says Smith, is to become aware of our immersions. We need a "liturgical audit" of our day-to-day and week-to-week habits to see which stories we are absorbed in and what they're doing to woo our hearts, capture our minds, and shape our imaginations. Where are you getting your stories during the majority of the week? What do these stories want you to worship? Who do they want you to love?

The second step, I would say, is to continually immerse ourselves in the Christian story that reorients us to the deepest, truest version of reality. There are numerous, important ways to do this, not the least of which is regular participation in corporate Christian worship.[24]

But this is a book about the Bible, so I'm going to talk about the Bible. If we're going to stand up to the stories told by the world, we need to be rooted in the story found in Scripture, revolving around Christ. If we claim to follow Jesus, we need to be immersed in the story where he is the hero, where God is constantly acting to save, and where the ultimate orientation of the cosmos is toward hope.

"The church's story has one intent: *to shape the identity of God's people, and therefore every one of God's people*," says Scot McKnight.[25] When the Bible's narrative seeps down into our bones, both individually and in our communities, it reinforces the core essence of our identity: that we are God's image bearers, deeply broken yet infinitely loved. It remakes us into beings who are more truly human, who look and act more like Christ. And it invites us into God's mission to bring restoration to all creation.

The false stories and promises of the world will never go away. They will regularly seduce us, tempt us, and sometimes ensnare us in their lies and half-truths. But if we constantly return to the story of Scripture, which subverts and deflects the alternative stories, we will know when we've been lured away from Home and return to the One who gives us true life.

↻

I've spilled quite a bit of ink in this chapter about why understanding the Bible as the defining grand narrative of the world is so critical to reading it well. But if this concept is still new to you, you may be wondering, *Okay, but what the heck is the story?*

"Christian theology is about knowing the story, its plot, the characters, the protagonist, the villains, the struggle, and the resolution," says Wright. "And then—most of all—knowing the church's place, within that story, the ongoing act of the divine drama."[26]

Next up on our journey is a bird's-eye tour of the six-act drama of Scripture, from Genesis to Revelation.

The Six-Act Drama of Scripture

I will explain. No, it is too much. I will sum up.
INIGO MONTOYA, *THE PRINCESS BRIDE*

WHEN MY WIFE AND I were on our honeymoon in Paris, we spent an afternoon exploring near the Eiffel Tower. As one of the world's most recognizable structures (and most unavoidable tourist destinations) we were drawn closer and closer until, finally, we were standing underneath it. We craned our necks up at the massive iron spire and then looked over and saw the number of people in line for the elevators to the observation deck. "Is it worth it?" we asked. We were only in Paris for a few days, and the wait to get to the top would take up valuable pastry-eating time.

Eventually we decided that the bird's-eye view of one of the world's most beautiful cities was worth the wait. When we finally got to the top, we slowly circled the observation deck and absorbed the city. The Champ de Mars spread out before us like an enormous green carpet, the Seine meandered its way through the gray rooftops, and the stark white Sacré-Cœur Basilica stared back at us from its perch on the hill to the northeast.

There's something about a high-level vantage point that helps you get to know a place, to see the big picture of how its numerous components come together into a comprehensive whole. In chapter 4, we explored how reading big helps us zoom out from the verses and take in the overarching message of an entire book of the Bible. Now we're going to zoom out even further to see how all the Bible's books work together to tell one overarching narrative about God, humanity, evil, Jesus, and the restoration of all things.

Over the years, a number of frameworks and models for understanding the Bible's grand narrative have been proposed, and many of them are very good. The model that has been most helpful to me is to look at Scripture as a six-act drama that begins in Genesis and previews the ending in Revelation.

As with any bird's-eye view, it will be impossible to capture all the intricacies, themes, depth, and meaning of the Bible's story. We truly get to know the Bible at ground level, walking its streets, looking in its windows, and sitting in its sidewalk cafés, simply soaking it all in. But it's also extremely helpful to have a mental map handy to locate ourselves within the big story, no matter where we're reading. So let's dive in.

Act 1: God Makes a Temple

"In the beginning God created the heavens and the earth. Now the earth was formless and empty, darkness was over the surface of the deep, and the Spirit of God was hovering over the waters."[1]

Most everybody is familiar with the first sentence of the Bible, but we have a habit of skimming over the second sentence as we hurry to "Let there be light."[2] What's all this about "formless and empty" but also having deep waters?

The ancient Israelites (like many other ancient societies) believed that the raw material of the cosmos was an untamed, swirling, throbbing watery chaos. Throughout Scripture, whether it's the Red Sea crushing the Egyptians or the Sea of Galilee threatening to drown Jesus and his disciples, bodies of water are portrayed as chaotic and unpredictable—vestiges of the disordered and violent origins of the universe.

So the opening story of Genesis introduces us to a Creator who organizes the formlessness and fills the emptiness.

During days one, two, and three of the Creation story, God makes the necessary distinctions that bring order and form to the cosmos. He creates light to counter the darkness. He pushes back the waters of the heavens from the waters of the earth and calls the space between *sky*. He causes the waters underneath the sky to bunch up so that dry land can emerge. Vegetation springs up from the land—plants and trees that bear seeds and produce their own fruit.

"On day one God created the basis for time; day two the basis for weather; and day three the basis for food," says John Walton. "These three great functions—time, weather and food—are the foundation of life."[3]

During days four, five, and six, God fills what he has formed. He places the sun, moon, and stars in the heavens to govern the day and night as well as the seasons and years. Then he creates birds and underwater creatures to occupy the sky and the sea and then animals to walk on land.

All these things God does in the first six days he declares *good*. They are good because they are drawn from him, the ultimate source of goodness, wisdom, order, and purpose. He has created function from the nonfunctional, pushing back the forces of chaos and making a world teeming with life that operates well. The whole earth is a declaration and reflection of his glory.

At the end of day six, God gathers dust from the ground and breathes life into it, creating *adam* (man) from *adamah* (ground). God sees that it is not good for the man to be alone, so he creates the woman as a strong and capable companion. These creatures are different from all the other earthly elements God has created, and God gives them a special blessing and a unique vocation. Humans receive the whole earth—every swimming, flying, and walking creature and every seed-bearing plant—to rule on God's behalf. This, God declares, is *very good*. On the seventh day, he rests from his work.

All right, so what are we supposed to get out of this story? The first couple of pages of the Bible are full of richness and meaning, and they have been the subject of enormous amounts of writing, speaking, and debate. But there are a few often-overlooked elements that introduce some of the Bible's most crucial themes, and the key to uncovering them lies quietly at the very end of the Creation story.

Walton comments that God's rest on the seventh day can be a bit mystifying: "It appears to be nothing more than an afterthought with theological concerns about Israelites observing the sabbath—an appendix, a postscript, a tack on."[4]

But God's rest, it turns out, reveals that this opening act of creation is a *temple-making story*.

In the ancient world, when deities "rested," it meant that they took up residence in their temple (see Psalm 132 and its references to "dwelling place" and "resting place"). "Rest is what results when a crisis has been resolved or when stability has been achieved, when things have 'settled down,'" says Walton.[5]

Imagine going through the process of building a house. First you lay the foundation, erect the walls, and build the roof (days one through three). Then you fill the house with appliances, furniture, artwork, and perhaps other people to share the home with you (days four through six). Finally, you walk into the house, pull up a chair, exhale, and smile with satisfaction. This is home.

The seventh day of Creation shows us that God's original intention was for heaven and earth to be one and the same, overlapping and interlocking realms where the Creator would live with his creation. His control center for running the cosmos would not be "out there" in the ether but right here among the trees and birds and, most importantly, his children.

All this brings us to the second major takeaway from this temple-making story: the image bearers. A universal feature in ancient temples was the presence of a statue (or image) that acted as a physical expression of the unseen god who resided in the temple. In the Genesis story, however, God's image is not carved out of wood or stone. It is made of flesh and bone.

The Hebrew word for "image" is *tselem*, which in Greek is *eikon*. These human eikons, much like the idols of ancient temples, play a representative role. They are not only set apart from the rest of the created order—they are somehow *like God*.

Oftentimes, that's where the conversation ends. We know that bearing God's image means we somehow, mysteriously, represent his character and qualities to the world. That's certainly true, but it's only part of the story. The part that often gets left out is that we're also made to represent his *purposes*. Scot McKnight explains:

> To be an Eikon means, first of all, to be in union with God as Eikons; second, it means to be in communion with other Eikons; and third, it means to *participate* with God in his creating, his ruling, his speaking, his naming, his ordering, his variety and beauty, his location, his partnering, and his resting, and to oblige God in his obligating of us.[6]

Humans are God's images, but we are also given a mandate *to image*: to reflect God's glory into creation like an angled mirror, to go forth and steward the earth on his behalf. This is our fundamental human vocation, and it is vital to the story.

As God came to dwell on the earth with his image bearers, creation was filled with his *shalom*. Peace, wholeness, and deep relational harmony flowed in every direction. Humans had shalom with God, with one another, within themselves, and with the earth.

And for about five seconds, everything was as it should be.

Act 2: Rebellion

In the middle of the Garden of Eden are two trees: the tree of life and the tree of the knowledge of good and evil. When God places the humans in the Garden to cultivate and care for it, he tells them they are free to eat from any tree in the Garden, including the tree of life. There's just one exception:

"You are free to eat from any tree in the garden; but you must not eat from the tree of the knowledge of good and evil, for when you eat from it you will certainly die."[7]

God gives humans the dignity of a choice. They can choose to trust God's definition of good and evil, or they can choose to disobey him and take the authority to define good and evil for themselves. They can yield to God and eat from his tree of life, or they can find their own way by eating from the tree that promises false life.

"An idea is like a virus," says Leonardo DiCaprio in the movie *Inception*. "Resilient. Highly contagious. And the smallest seed of an idea can grow. It can grow to define or destroy you."[8]

A serpent slithers onto the scene and offers Eve a simple idea: *Maybe God is holding out on you.* "You will not certainly die," it hisses. "For God knows that when you eat from it your eyes will be opened, and you will be like God, knowing good and evil."[9]

"The serpent subtly casts doubt on God's words to Adam and Eve and doubt even on God's inherent goodness," write Craig Bartholomew and Michael Goheen. "It suggests that God is *afraid* that his human creatures might become his equals once they know good and evil."[10]

When God's image bearers take a bite of the forbidden fruit, a shalom-breaking shock wave is sent out in every direction. Suddenly perceiving their nakedness, they are consumed with shame. They experience the clutching sensation of fear for the first time and quickly hide from their Maker. When they're questioned about what they've done, the man points his finger and blames the woman.

God explains that because of their rebellion, their mandate to fill the earth and care for it will now be riddled with resistance and hardship. Childbirth will be difficult and painful. The land that used to voluntarily burst forth with life is now cursed. It will fight against Adam, and his work will turn from joyful cultivation into sweaty toil. Humankind is now subject to death and will return to the dust from which it came. Under these circumstances, human beings can no longer dwell with God in his temple, this sacred place where heaven and earth overlap. Adam and Eve are exiled from the Garden.

From there, things spiral out of control. Cain murders his brother Abel; eikons made to be cocreators with God have reversed course and begun destroying life instead. Generations pass, and God's heart breaks more and more: "The LORD saw how great the wickedness of the human race had become on the earth, and that every inclination of the thoughts of the human heart was only evil all the time."[11] Rebellion has overtaken the world, and God regrets ever making the human race.

He lets loose the primordial waters of chaos to overtake the earth once more. Rain pours from the sky, and the springs open up from the earth, wiping out every living thing. Only Noah, his family, and the creatures on the ark are spared. The entire creation project is hanging by a thread.

When the waters subside, God makes a promise. "Never again," he tells Noah.[12] He hangs his bow in the sky (the same word used to describe a bow that fires arrows) and vows that never again will he wash the stage of this cosmic drama. From now on, he will work with humans to defeat the evil that has infiltrated his good creation. He will accommodate our brokenness, our stubbornness, and our constant rebellion. His love will overcome it all.

Act 3: Israel's Calling

After Noah's story finishes, we're met with a few paragraphs of genealogies. "The descendants of Shem were Elam, Asshur, Arphaxad, Lud, and Aram. The descendants of Aram were Uz, Hul, Gether, and Mash."[13] Not exactly riveting narrative, but if you're looking for baby name ideas . . . well . . . they're all awful.

Lots of time passes. Hundreds of years. Where is this story going? It feels stuck in neutral. Finally, God makes his move.

Throughout Scripture, we see that God likes to start small and work slow, often in the unlikeliest of places. After centuries of silence, he chooses a seventy-five-year-old, childless desert nomad named Abram (whose name is later changed to Abraham) and declares that he will be the seed for humanity's renewal and creation's restoration.

> I will make you into a great nation,
>   and I will bless you;
> I will make your name great,
>   and you will be a blessing.
> I will bless those who bless you,
>   and whoever curses you I will curse;
> *and all peoples on earth*
>   *will be blessed through you.*[14]

God's restoration project for the entire earth begins with one man and his family. As Gordon Wenham explains:

> [Abraham], like Noah before him, is a second Adam
> figure. Adam was given the garden of Eden: Abraham

is promised the land of Canaan. God told Adam to be
fruitful and multiply: Abraham is promised descendants
as numerous as the stars of heaven. God walked with
Adam in Eden: Abraham was told to walk before God.
In this way the advent of Abraham is seen as the answer
to the problems set out in Genesis 1–11: through him
all the families of the earth will be blessed.[15]

Jumping ahead a few hundred more years: Abraham's family
has indeed grown into a great nation. But they're in trouble:
enslaved to the Egyptians and outside the land they've been promised. God's covenant with Abraham is only half fulfilled. How is
this nation supposed to go forth and bless the world if they're stuck
stomping mud into bricks, generation after generation?

God works with Moses, the nation's new leader, to rescue
his people from the evil tyrant Pharaoh. He brings forth plagues
that decimate the Egyptians, showcasing his power over creation
through his defeat of the Egyptian gods. Israel's exodus from Egypt
is the defining moment of their national history, deeply formative
for their corporate identity. They remember God's rescue from
oppression and slavery every year with the Feast of the Passover, a
celebration that will return with great significance later in the story.

Moses leads the people into the wilderness, to Mount Sinai. They
are a rescued people, and now they are to become a dedicated nation.
"You yourselves have seen what I did to Egypt, and how I carried you
on eagles' wings and brought you to myself," says God. "Now if you
obey me fully and keep my covenant, then out of all nations you will
be my treasured possession. Although the whole earth is mine, you
will be for me a kingdom of priests and a holy nation."[16]

The Israelites are to be a set-apart people, fundamentally different from the surrounding nations. They are called to showcase to the world who God is and what it looks like to have shalom with him. They're to live faithfully and obediently under his rule and to reflect his glory into all creation. Through this family of Abraham, God will call the entire world back to himself.

They're given the Mosaic law, which outlines the details of this covenant relationship. The law giving constitutes a very long, tedious, strange, and sometimes unsettling portion of the Old Testament, and it's where many people lose steam when trying to read through the Bible. But it shows that God is serious about his people living differently from the other nations. The circumstances are not perfect by any means, but many of the instructions we find alarming (like the perspective on slaves and women) are actually steps toward justice and redemption when compared to the law codes of the surrounding ancient people groups. God starts small and works slow. He meets us where we are.

Toward the end of Exodus, we find a long section containing God's extremely detailed instructions for building the Tabernacle and then, a short while later, a repetition of those instructions as Israel actually builds it. This is another passage that feels long and tedious, but if we look carefully, we can see that it is packed with parallels to the opening Creation story of Genesis. The implications are clear: God earnestly wants to dwell with his people once again. If the whole cosmos is rotten with sin and evil, unfit to contain his glory, then a portable tent will suffice for now.

So here we are. God has planted the seed for new beginnings, and now the question is whether the seed will grow and blossom or wither and die.

The rest of Act 3 (most of the Old Testament) contains the up-and-down, back-and-forth story of Israel's attempts to live into their Sinai-given vocation. God has set them apart to be a light to the world, yet they, too, are infected with sin. Their long national history in Samuel–Kings narrates the nation's struggle to uphold their end of the covenant and be the people God has called them to be. Good kings come and lead them into righteousness and fidelity to the Lord. Then evil kings come, and they descend into idolatry and injustice.

During their best years, under King David and King Solomon, Israel grows into a flourishing nation. Jerusalem is strong and beautiful, and the name of Israel's God is known to the surrounding peoples. Solomon builds a magnificent Temple, and God's presence comes to dwell in the middle of the city.

But it doesn't last. The prophets yell and scream for the people to repent and return to the Lord their God, but they don't listen. Their eyes are darkened by the sin that courses through their veins. Their necks are stiff; their hearts are hard. God's holy nation is no different from the pagan nations—just as immoral, just as violent, just as exploitative.

Eventually, as in Eden, God chooses to exile his people. The Babylonians come and level Jerusalem. God's presence departs from the Temple, and it is destroyed. The people are taken away from the Promised Land and into exile in Babylon.

The Old Testament ends in uncertainty. The Israelites eventually return to Jerusalem and rebuild the Temple, but it's a disappointment compared to the first one. There is no record of God's presence filling it as it had Solomon's Temple. The nation is back in the Promised Land, yet the land means little if God is not there with them. As Israel comes to terms with their enduring exile from the presence of God, they're faced with big questions. Has God abandoned his promises, or will he stand by them? Will he send a King to heal the nation and lead them back into their holy vocation? Is he still going to rescue the world?

Act 4: The Upside-Down Victory of the Unexpected Messiah

It's easy for us to turn from the last page of the Old Testament to the first page of the New Testament without thinking of the four hundred years that passed between the two. Four hundred years of questioning, of silence, of waiting. Four hundred years of subjugation, rebellions, and the disappointment that always came with the deaths of those who seemed like the hoped-for Messiah. The people are weary, yet their eyes are always on the horizon, longing for the Lord to act.

God starts small and works slow. This time he starts with one cell, then two, then four, eight, sixteen. "Do not be afraid, Mary; you have found favor with God," the angel Gabriel tells the frightened teenager. "You will conceive and give birth to a son, and you are to call him Jesus. He will be great and will be called the Son of the Most High. The Lord God will give him the throne of his father David, and he will reign over Jacob's descendants forever; his kingdom will never end."[17]

The Son of the Most High enters the world in a lowly place surrounded by humble people. God has come again to dwell with his people, astonishingly, *in the flesh*. No temples or tabernacles, but as one of them. For thirty years, he lives and works in complete obscurity, waiting for his time to come.

Splash, splash, splash. John the Baptist appears to prepare the way for the King. He preaches in the wilderness, calling the people to repentance and the forgiveness of sins and then descends into the Jordan River to baptize them. More than a thousand years earlier, Israel crossed this same river on their way into the Promised Land. This is a place of new beginnings, a place to recover the vocation to be a light to the nations.

Jesus comes from Nazareth to be baptized by John. "Though he (unlike the others) does not need to be cleansed from sin, he identifies himself with the nation, taking on himself their mission to become the channel of God's salvation to the nations," say Bartholomew and Goheen.[18] God's Spirit descends and empowers him for his mission. A voice speaks from heaven: "You are my Son, whom I love; with you I am well pleased."[19]

Jesus launches his ministry with the core theme of *euangelion*: the Greek word for "good news." In the first century, a messenger might come running into town with *euangelion* of a military victory, or a new ruler might issue a decree announcing the *euangelion* of his reign.

"Good news!" says Jesus. "The kingdom of God has arrived." The long exile is over. God has kept his promises to Noah, Abraham, Moses, and David. He is becoming King again, returning to bring freedom, forgiveness, redemption, and renewal to a hurting world.

Jesus travels around Galilee, teaching about this new kingdom and showing what it looks like. The kingdom of heaven is like a farmer who planted good seed in his field; the kingdom of heaven is like a mustard seed; the kingdom of heaven is like a treasure that a man discovered hidden in a field; the kingdom of heaven is like a fishing net thrown into the water. Blessed are the poor in spirit, the meek, the merciful, the peacemakers, those who hunger and thirst for righteousness. This kingdom certainly operates differently from the kingdoms of the world. There is much to learn. Much to change.

He heals the sick and the lame, forgives sins, raises the dead. He overpowers the dark forces that have been enslaving God's people, casting out demons and restoring the captives to their full humanity. His miracles are not merely proof that he is God, as they have so often been reduced to. They are signposts, foretastes of what it looks like for God's purposes to be fully realized on earth as in heaven.

Everywhere he goes, Jesus defies the expectations of Israel's religious leaders. He eats and drinks with tax collectors and sinners. He works on the Sabbath. He doesn't display the strength needed to overthrow Rome and retake Jerusalem but instead chooses a life of suffering, service, and self-giving love. Certainly this stonemason from Nazareth cannot be the Messiah. He's doing it all wrong.

The religious leaders' refusals of Jesus' kingdom announcements turn his words of welcome into words of warning. Israel's leaders have a long history of rejecting God's messengers—will they also reject God himself? Jesus continually rebukes them for their self-righteousness and their separatist way of life. Tensions rise as he journeys closer and closer to Jerusalem, the headquarters of the religious establishment.

On the road to Jerusalem, Jesus tells his disciples exactly what is about to happen: "The Son of Man will be delivered over to the chief priests and the teachers of the law. They will condemn him to death and will hand him over to the Gentiles, who will mock him and spit on him, flog him and kill him. Three days later he will rise."[20]

For the disciples, this news simply doesn't compute. "Yeah, um, sure," say James and John. "But when you're crowned king, can we sit at your right and left hand?" The Messiah's job is to fight Israel's battles. His closest followers still think he's going to Jerusalem to defeat Rome through force, take back the land for God's people, and rule the way kings have always ruled. But the battle Jesus is going to fight is bigger than they could ever imagine, and his way of fighting it is more implausible than they could ever expect.

He enters Jerusalem and begins making a ruckus. He overturns the tables in the Temple and condemns the chief priests and Pharisees. Tensions continue to rise, and those in power begin looking for ways to kill him.

All four Gospels make a point to mention that Jesus' final days took place during the Passover celebration. This, many scholars argue, is not a coincidence. "Jesus chose to go to Jerusalem and (so it seems) force some kind of a showdown with the authorities not on the Day of Atonement, not at the Festival of Tabernacles, the Festival of Dedication, or any other special day on the sacred calendar . . . but at Passover," says N. T. Wright.[21]

"He chose, for his final and fateful symbolic confrontation with Jerusalem and its authorities, the moment when all his fellow Jews were busy celebrating the Exodus from Egypt and praying that God would do again, only on a grander scale, what he had done all those years ago."[22]

And so it's with this backdrop that we come to the climax of the entire biblical narrative. Jesus is taken to the cross to enact a new exodus, except this time freedom is won by losing. Jesus' sacrificial and substitutionary death on the cross is somehow, mysteriously, the key not only to sapping Rome of its power but also to undermining the dark forces, principalities, and powers of sin and death that hold all humanity captive.

The Cross is the end of the exile. It's the forgiveness of sins. It's the reconciliation of humanity with God. It's freedom from our bondage to sin and death. It's the coronation of the King and the beginning of the installation of God's kingdom on earth as it is in heaven.

Of course, nobody knows it at the time, save perhaps for one Roman centurion. As much as Jesus of Nazareth seemed like the right guy, all anyone else sees is another failed Messiah. The disciples scatter in terror. Jesus' limp and bloody body is taken away and sealed in a tomb. Silence.

On Sunday, the women head to the tomb only to find it empty. Their panic quickly turns to wide-eyed hope as they hear the Good News for the first time. "Why do you look for the living among the dead? He is not here; he has risen!"[23] Jesus' upside-down victory over sin and death has been validated by the Father. He is the firstborn of the resurrection, the firstfruits of a new creation.

John gives us a different account of the scene at the tomb. Mary Magdalene sees Jesus but doesn't recognize him, mistaking him for the gardener. (I always wonder if the resurrected Christ walked out of the tomb and started pulling weeds.) The symbolism is thick here: John opened his Gospel with "In the beginning . . . ," calling the reader back to the first words of Genesis.

Now at the end of the story we're reminded of Adam, the first gardener. But this is a new day, and a new Gardener has come to tend to the earth.

Jesus appears to his disciples, simultaneously hard to recognize and also fully himself. He shows them his scars and shares breakfast with them on the beach, and they see that this is indeed their friend Jesus, in the flesh. There's just something different, something *new*.

"All authority in heaven and on earth has been given to me," he tells them. "Therefore go and make disciples of all nations, baptizing them in the name of the Father and of the Son and of the Holy Spirit, and teaching them to obey everything I have commanded you."[24]

Jesus has become King of the cosmos, but he will not assert his rule through violence and coercion. Instead, he reaffirms the way in which he carried out his mission on earth: The kingdom will grow through the tender, messy process of making disciples. "Through the unpretentious and humble mission of the church in making disciples, the exalted Christ, the Lord with all authority, will 'subdue' his enemies—in love."[25]

With the final line in Matthew's Gospel, Jesus closes the curtain on Act 4 and sets the stage for Act 5: "And surely I am with you always, to the very end of the age."[26]

Act 5: The Already and the Not Yet

The first page of the book of Acts tells us that Jesus remains on earth for a time. He appears to his disciples, "and he proved to them in many ways that he was actually alive."[27] He talks with them about the kingdom of God and reaffirms his promise that the Father's gift is coming. His Spirit—their Helper—will come upon them and enable them to be witnesses to everything they have seen. Then, triumphantly, Jesus ascends to be with the Father.

On the day of Pentecost, the Spirit does indeed come and settle on Jesus' followers. In a wild scene, a loud sound like a violent wind fills the house they are in, and what look like tongues of fire come to rest on each of them. They begin speaking in a number of languages they have never learned, showing that the *euangelion* of Jesus isn't limited to the immediate geographic area. This is news that needs to be spread far and wide.

And what exactly is the news? Peter stands up in front of a crowd on Pentecost and tells them the story of Jesus of Nazareth. He finishes by saying, "God has raised this Jesus to life, and we are all witnesses of it. Exalted to the right hand of God, he has received from the Father the promised Holy Spirit and has poured out what you now see and hear. . . . Therefore let all Israel be assured of this: God has made this Jesus, whom you crucified, both Lord and Messiah."[28]

Jesus is risen. Jesus is Lord. Seated at the right hand of God, he has been given all authority, honor, and glory. "Jesus does not merely sit on the throne of our hearts and reign there," say Bartholomew and Goheen. "That is much too narrow a concept of his authority. Jesus reigns over *all* of human life, all history, and all nations."[29]

So here's the thing: If you were a Jew in the first century, your worldview was built on the basis of two time periods—the *present evil age*, dominated by exile, evil, sin, and death, and the *age to come*, when God returns to Israel and establishes his kingdom on earth as in heaven. In the Jewish mindset, the transition between these two ages would be immediate, like flipping a light switch.

It turns out, though, that the kingdom of God is more like a dimmer switch. The message preached by the apostles is that although death, evil, and injustice still fill our world, the age to come has indeed arrived. Jesus' resurrection launched a new world right in the middle of the old one.

The book of Acts shows us how the earliest communities of Jesus followers wrap their minds around this new reality and step into it. The same Spirit who descended on Jesus at the Jordan River has been poured out on them, dwelling within each of them and among all of them, uniting them in fellowship and empowering them for the mission of God. Beginning in Jerusalem and spreading outward into Judea, Samaria, and eventually into Rome itself, the first Christians spread the Good News. They cannot help but speak about what they've seen and heard.

Following Acts (in the traditional book order), the rest of the New Testament consists of letters to these early churches. Although the letters are not narrative in form, they certainly contribute to the story of the Bible. We see that the first believers need help understanding the deep intricacies and implications of the gospel. They need encouragement in the midst of persecution and guidance for how to faithfully operate a Jesus-centered community.

The letters of Peter, Paul, and the other apostles show us that life as the body of Christ is often messy and hard and that Jesus was serious when he told his followers to pick up their crosses and follow him. The post-Jesus church straddles two worlds, living in the already-and-not-yet kingdom of God.

Act 5 of the grand narrative is where Christ's church finds itself today—in this time between Christ's ascension and his return to bring God's kingdom to earth in all its fullness. Two thousand years after the Resurrection, the Holy Spirit still dwells in and among those who profess faith in Jesus. We continue forward in the legacy left by the New Testament churches, carrying forth the restorative, healing gospel, which declares that Christ is King. This renewed vocation will be the focus of the final chapter of this book.

Act 6: God Comes Home

If you're familiar with the Marvel movies that dominated box offices from 2008 to 2019, you know all about the famous post-credit scenes. When the latest Iron Man or Captain America blockbuster faded to black, moviegoers didn't empty out of the theaters as usual. Instead, we waited around for ten minutes while the credits rolled because we knew we couldn't miss the last little piece of Marvel storytelling that would flash on screen when the credits ended.

Sometimes, the tiny, one-minute vignettes were meaningless and funny, like when the team of Avengers was shown silently munching on shawarma in a hole-in-the-wall restaurant following an intergalactic melee in Manhattan. But as the Marvel Cinematic Universe grew and the overarching plot thickened, the post-credit scenes offered critical clues about where the writers and producers were going to take the story next.

Act 6 of the biblical narrative is kind of like that. It is oriented toward the future, pointing forward to a time when Jesus will return and finish his fight against all that has corrupted God's good creation. The Bible doesn't lay out scene-by-scene descriptions of these future events but relies on hints and allusions to give us a sense of how the story ends. Before we explore the end, though, we need to return to the beginning.

In the beginning, remember, God pushed back the darkness and disorder to make room for light and life. He knit atoms together into trees and water and birds and then breathed life into his image bearers. All this, he declared, was good and very good. His temple was beautiful and filled with his shalom. It was his pleasure to dwell in it.

The long and winding story of the Bible is about God working to restore what was ruined by rebellion. So why do we so often believe that the story ends with him burning it all up?

For centuries, the most popular version of the Christian narrative has concluded with God destroying the earth and plucking his chosen people away to live out eternity with him in a spiritual, disembodied heaven. This view of the "afterlife" and the ultimate destiny of the world has shaped our theology, guided our ethics, and animated our imaginations. And it's simply incongruent with what the New Testament actually says.

There's not nearly enough space to go into all the details here (see N. T. Wright's *Surprised by Hope* and J. Richard Middleton's *A New Heaven and a New Earth* for fuller explorations), but from the Prophets to Jesus to Peter to Paul to Revelation, the theme is consistent: The biblical story is not about escape to heaven from earth; it's about the reunification of heaven and earth.

When Jesus teaches his disciples to pray, he tells them to ask God that his kingdom will come "on earth as it is in heaven."[30] He speaks in Matthew about the "renewal of all things,"[31] which Peter echoes in Acts when he mentions "the time for the final restoration of all things, as God promised long ago through his holy prophets."[32] When from the cross Jesus utters "It is finished,"[33] he is declaring that this redemption is here. The wheels are in motion. God is reclaiming his good creation.

Paul continues this theme in his letters, perhaps most notably in the beginning of his letter to the Colossians:

> The Son is the image of the invisible God, the firstborn over all creation. For in him all things were created: things in heaven and on earth, visible and invisible, whether thrones or powers or rulers or authorities; all things have been created through him and for him. He is before all things, and in him all things hold together. And he is the head of the body, the church; he is the beginning and the firstborn from among the dead, so that in everything he might have the supremacy. For God was pleased to have all his fullness dwell in him, *and through him to reconcile to himself all things*, whether things on earth or things in heaven, by making peace through his blood, shed on the cross.[34]

If Jesus is Lord over everything, then everything is within his domain to fix and restore. "All things" means *all things*.

Finally, the book of Revelation gives us a picture of what this redemption and reconciliation will look like:

> Then I saw "a new heaven and a new earth," for the first heaven and the first earth had passed away, and there was no longer any sea. I saw the Holy City, the

new Jerusalem, coming down out of heaven from God, prepared as a bride beautifully dressed for her husband. And I heard a loud voice from the throne saying, "Look! God's dwelling place is now among the people, and he will dwell with them. They will be his people, and God himself will be with them and be their God. 'He will wipe every tear from their eyes. There will be no more death' or mourning or crying or pain, for the old order of things has passed away."

He who was seated on the throne said, "I am making everything new!" Then he said, "Write this down, for these words are trustworthy and true."[35]

The final vision is not of souls flying away to heaven as the earth burns up but of *resurrection and new creation.* Scripture does say there will be a time of judgment and fire, but God's judgment makes things straight that were once crooked. His fire refines and purifies, melting away the dross to reveal a place fit to receive its Creator. Heaven and earth—God's realm and our realm—will be one and the same, and God will dwell with his people once again. The ending of the story isn't actually an ending at all but a new beginning.

The point of Act 6 is that God doesn't abandon his creation project. He doesn't admit that, on second thought, maybe it wasn't such a good idea after all. God gets what he wants, and what he declared good in the beginning will be made good again.

Act 6 helps us see how Jesus' work in the present is tied to his final vision for the future. Getting this part of the story right allows us to go forth into a confused and hurting world with a message of hope—a message not of evacuation but of restoration. "There really is a different way to be human, and it has been decisively launched with Jesus," says Wright.[36] Freed from the bonds of sin and death, and empowered by the Spirit, we can once again begin to image God, however imperfectly, in ways that point forward to a time when sin and death will be no more, when the whole earth will be filled with his shalom.

New Creation Improv

Therefore, if anyone is in Christ, the new creation has come:
The old has gone, the new is here!
THE APOSTLE PAUL

WHEN I WAS ELEVEN YEARS OLD, *The Fellowship of the Ring*, the first movie from The Lord of the Rings trilogy, was released in theaters. Within a few minutes of the opening scene, I was hooked. The series drew me into the story of Frodo Baggins, the unlikeliest of heroes, as he struggled through an epic journey from his home in the Shire across Middle-earth to Mordor to destroy the Ring of Power. This little, curly-haired hobbit with a heavy gold ring strung around his neck was the world's only hope to defeat the imminent threat of doom.

My siblings and I grew up on these movies. We bought the games, reenacted the scenes, and staged battles of all sorts in our backyard. Anytime we were home sick from school and curled up on the couch, the biggest question was which one of the three DVDs would go into the player.

It wasn't until my early twenties, though, that I sat down and actually read The Lord of the Rings books published by J. R. R. Tolkien in the 1950s. And I was stunned to learn that the books actually have a different ending.

In the movies, the Ring of Power is cast into the volcanic fire of Mount Doom—the only place in Middle-earth that can destroy it—and Sauron's evil empire immediately crumbles. The orcs and trolls who comprised his massive army scatter and die. The threat is extinguished, and the trilogy winds down with a deep sense of satisfaction and redemption.

In the books, however, the ending is not so simple. After destroying the Ring, Frodo and his companions return to the green hills of the Shire only to discover that, in their absence, their home has been overtaken by a horde of ruffians. The once bright and cheerful villages have a gloom and foulness about them: "Through rows of new mean houses along each side of the road, they saw the new mill in all its frowning and dirty ugliness: a great brick building straddling the stream, which it fouled with a steaming and stinking outflow. All along the Bywater Road every tree had been felled."[1]

Aghast, the hobbits immediately set to work ridding the Shire of the troublemakers and their leaders, who have turned their beautiful home into a desolate place. Once they drive out the bad actors, they take a moment to survey the work still needing to be done.

"And that's the end of that," said Sam. "A nasty end, and I wish I needn't have seen it; but it's a good riddance."

"And the very last end of the War, I hope," said
Merry. . . .

"I shan't call it the end, till we've cleared up the mess,"
said Sam gloomily. "And that'll take a lot of time and
work."[2]

They free the prisoners who have been held captive in dark
and narrow cells, replant saplings where trees have been felled, and
repair broken storefront windows. They tear down the offensive
buildings that were erected in their absence and use the bricks to
make their old homes snugger and drier. It does indeed take time
and work, as Sam predicts, but in due time the Shire once again
bursts forth with trees and flowers and fruit.

As followers of Jesus in the fifth act of the biblical narrative,
we find ourselves today in a similar place as Frodo and his friends.
Christ has won the decisive victory on the cross, disarming and
defeating Satan and his company of dark forces, who have tres-
passed into God's good creation. The Ring of Power, so to speak,
has been destroyed. And yet the story is not over.

Instead, we live in the in-between time, straddling the old,
dark world and the new creation, which will be filled with
Christ's light. Like the hobbits who know the good news of evil's
defeat, we are still confronted with the stark realities of our time:
of ruffians and troublemakers, brokenness and sorrow, ugliness
and captivity.

It's in the tension of this dual reality that we glimpse one of
the Bible's most stunning characteristics. Earlier in our journey
together we moved away from the concept of the Bible as a pot-
pourri of encouragement, rules, propositions, and theological bullet

points and toward the idea that it's a unified story centered on Jesus. Now we must take one more step, moving from story to *drama*.

God uses Scripture to tell us the story *so far*, to show us how he has been working throughout history to reclaim his good creation and how that work has culminated in the life, ministry, death, and resurrection of the Messiah. Now he invites us to enter into that story.

Biblical Improvisation

Imagine, says N. T. Wright, that someone discovered a long-lost drama written by Shakespeare that had never been seen or performed before. As she reads through the script, she determines that it's unmistakably Shakespeare, but to her dismay, she realizes that the drama is unfinished. The first four acts are there, as well as the first scene from the fifth act, but the page is torn, and the rest of the play is missing.

What should she do with this discovery? She could put the papers in a drawer and forget about them, or she could hire actors to read and perform the script as is with no attempt to finish the play. The best option, however, is to find actors who live and breathe Shakespeare, who are experts in his themes and style, to perform the first four acts *and then improvise the fifth*.

This is the life God is inviting us into through the Bible. Its story is not merely one we read and observe but one we enter and perform—a drama that we improvise in our own times and places.

"Our task is to discover, through the Spirit and prayer, the appropriate ways of improvising the script between the foundation events and the charter, on the one hand, and the complete coming of the Kingdom on the other. Once we grasp this framework, other things begin to fall into place," says Wright.[3]

For many people, seeing the word *improvise* anywhere near the Bible can create an uneasy feeling. We'd prefer the clarity and straightforward authority of a script. Read the Bible and do what it says—it's as simple as that. Except that it doesn't work that way.

Living as improv actors in the grand story of God's cosmos might sound somewhat untethered, but it's something we do every day whether we think of it in those terms or not. We don't roll out of bed in the morning, open our Bibles, and look up our lines for the day. We don't go to work and read verbatim off a divinely inspired script. In fact, we're implicitly aware that we can't find direct answers in the Bible to many of the questions and problems we face every day. We can't simply look up "biblical answers" for modern complexities like artificial intelligence, global pandemics, or representative democracies. It's not that kind of book.

Instead, God gives us the dignity and the responsibility of responding to the text by improvising lives that fit the thrust and direction of the story. We're the world's most significant creatures, made in the image of the Creator. Rational, emotional, spiritual, discerning, creative beings. Psalm 8 says that God made us a little lower than the angels, crowned us with glory and honor. Rulers over the creation. Not robots.

We don't take the stage of this drama alone or empty-handed either. The beauty of improvising the biblical story is that God is on the stage with us as both the Author and the Main Character in the story. It's not our responsibility to move the great cosmic drama forward but rather, through the Spirit, to play our supporting roles as faithfully as we can. And the Author has given us a number of things to help us on our way.

First off, we're surrounded on the stage by other broken, imperfect actors. The Spirit poured out on believers creates communities of fellow gospel improvisers, and God designed us to work together. Our faith community is both global and historic, unbound by time or geography, but it becomes most focused in the context of the local church. Our pastors serve as player-coaches, simultaneously enmeshed in the drama and helping us play our parts. The singing, prayer, Scripture reading, teaching, baptism, Eucharist, and other elements of our corporate worship help us regularly reorient ourselves to the deep realities of the drama we're in.

Second, of course, we have the gift of the Scriptures. The unfinished script reveals how God has crafted the trajectory of the story. It's a story with a mission, a story on the move. By constantly immersing ourselves in this narrative and allowing the Holy Spirit to speak, we absorb and internalize the character of the Author deep in our bones so that we can live into the story according to his intentions.

Finally, it's by grace that we're invited into the drama, and it's through grace that we're able to keep performing. The stage is saturated in forgiveness. The Author knows that we often don't play our parts very well, but he is patient and kind. The Spirit doesn't abandon us when we mess up. When we stumble, when we deliver lines that don't fit, when we allow ourselves to get caught up in rival stories, we are always invited back onstage to keep trying.

Discovering that the Bible contains a story—and that I am

invited into the story—was one of the most profoundly orienting experiences of my life. I had long been under the illusion that I was the hero of my own tale, that life was a movie about *me*, and that Scripture was useful insofar as I could find bits and pieces of it to fit into my personal drama. Of course, this approach wasn't working, because no human being is equipped to be the producer, director, and hero of their own story. It's not who we were made to be, as much as we like to fool ourselves into believing that we're capable.

Now I can see that the stage has never been my own but that the entirety of world history turns on the axis of Jesus. The pressure is off. I've been welcomed onto a grace-filled, love-soaked, Spirit-led, community-occupied stage to be remade in the image of Christ and participate in his work. The Bible is no longer a copy-and-paste instruction manual that I try to make room for in my busy life; rather, it's a conduit for the Spirit to form me and my community into better supporting actors within God's cosmic mission.

"In baptism, Christians are taken into a drama, where God has created them and others for a purpose, where Israel has answered a call and pursued a vocation, where Jesus has become one like them and has conquered sin and death, where the Spirit has empowered the church to follow Christ, and where God will end the drama in the fullness of time," says Samuel Wells. "Christians find their character by becoming a character in God's story."[4]

Creative Faithfulness

Considering all this, suddenly the Christian life moves from a mechanical spirituality to something more like art. Caught up in the invitation to respond to the Scriptures through our daily words and actions, we strive for lives that operate by a spirit of creative faithfulness to the story we find ourselves in.

Creative because God the Creator takes joy in our cocreating alongside him. He beckons us, his sinful yet redeemed image bearers, to imagine, build, think, explore, fix, play, and foster tiny pockets of shalom in our neighborhoods and communities. We are not inconsequential actors, merely rearranging deck chairs on a sinking ship. God is making all things new in Christ, and the fruit borne by his Spirit through his followers creates real beauty and restoration in the world. We bring our meager offerings to him to be transformed into something everlasting.

Faithfulness because it is easy to take the liberty of our creative calling and veer off course. We must be careful not to forget that we are supporting characters following the lead of Christ, and keeping our eyes on him requires a certain level of discipline. By returning constantly to the Scriptures and other tools, such as the historic creeds, we anchor ourselves to the mooring of our story and remember what it means to be the people of God. Our creative calling is grounded in obedience and sacrifice and humility. Daily life often requires us to simply follow the unsexy path of what Eugene Peterson calls "a long obedience in the same direction."[5]

All improvisational art works off of this mixture of creativity and faithfulness. Improv theater and improv comedy don't function unless the actors are willing to agree on a concept, take cues from one another, and then use their creativity to build upon one another's ideas and advance the performance. If the actors simply wait to be handed a script, the show doesn't go anywhere. If each actor insists on their own creative agenda, the show falls apart.

Jazz music, famous for its elements of improvisation, grows from the artists' deep commitment to the rules of music. If a quartet takes the stage with each member playing whatever they want in different keys and with varied tempos, the performance will be nothing but noise. Instead, the group works in harmony until the soloist branches off from the foundation of the song to create something familiar yet new. "In jazz, improvisation isn't a matter of just making any ol' thing up," says renowned trumpeter Wynton Marsalis. "Jazz, like any language, has its own grammar and vocabulary."[6]

Scripture sets the tone and tempo. The Psalms provide language and metaphor and emotion that help us live into life with God. The Prophets proclaim warnings and promises that still ring true today. Israel's exodus story shows us that we belong to a God who rescues. The Gospels reveal what God really looks like, how true love really works, and where the Creator is taking his creation project. Woven throughout the tapestry of these many books are consistent themes that reveal the character and mission of God, themes we must weave into our own lives as we improvise our roles today.

Finally, because the Bible is a story centered on Jesus, the best way we can exercise creative faithfulness to the story is to do so with the goal of becoming more like Jesus. As we read big and take in the grand narrative, we will notice that some things change over time. The story progresses, and we gain more clarity the closer we get to Jesus, the living Word, the true light in the darkness. In the Messiah, we have the clearest picture both of who God is and of what it means to be truly human. The Bible is not a flat book, where every sentence exists on equal footing, equally guiding us toward God's ideal vision for human flourishing. It's a story that is always curving toward Christ, so we have to interpret all Scripture in light of him. Some things don't line up with the person of Jesus, and other things find their fullest expression in him.

For example, most Christians know they can't quote "an eye for an eye" from Act 3 of the drama in order to justify their violent retaliation toward an attacker, because Jesus taught us to love and pray for our enemies. Women were regarded as little more than property early in the timeline represented in the Scriptures, yet Jesus repeatedly broke through the established norms to give them dignity and elevate their status. Early in the story, Israel moved God's purposes forward through warfare and conquest. But after Jesus, the first apostles spread the gospel through a subversive witness— undermining the ruling authorities with love and sacrifice.

On the other hand, the prophet Micah's exhortation to "act justly and to love mercy and to walk humbly with your God"[7] lines up well with Jesus' teachings. Jesus also affirms the greatest Old Testament commandments to "love the LORD your God with all your heart, all your soul, all your mind, and all your strength"[8] and to "love your neighbor as yourself."[9]

So improvising with creative faithfulness absolutely must involve evaluating every part of Scripture through the interpretive key of Jesus as the filter for how we play our parts in the drama. In some places, the gospel implications are clear; in other places, they will require us to wrestle with the text and discern through the Spirit how they play out in our modern lives.

What might this concept of creative faithfulness look like in real life? I believe it's as straightforward as using the gifts and passions the Creator has given us in order to bring the restoration and flourishing of the gospel into the world. Here in Colorado Springs, a former youth pastor named Mike Martin learned blacksmithing. Inspired by Isaiah's vision that "they will beat their swords into plowshares and their spears into pruning hooks,"[10] Martin and author Shane Claiborne cofounded RAWtools, an organization that accepts donated guns and literally beats them into gardening tools. In their forges, rifles and shotguns are refashioned into mattocks and spades.

RAWtools travels the country hosting events where family members of those slain by gun violence are invited to step up to the anvil and hammer away at the soft metal. For those whose hearts have been broken by these instruments of death, the act of transforming the steel into tools that cultivate life often moves them to tears.

The possibilities are vast and varied. Author Rosaria Butterfield has convincingly championed the lifestyle of "radically ordinary hospitality" and shares how she uses her gift of hospitality to open her home to strangers and neighbors alike.[11] Organizations like the Anselm Society and The Rabbit Room foster communities of Christian artists, providing places for holy imaginations to thrive and working to integrate art back into the life of the church. Over three hundred Christian rescue missions across the United States provide services to the hungry, homeless, abused, and addicted.[12]

"The characteristic common to God and man is apparently . . . the desire and the ability to make things," observed Dorothy Sayers.[13] For you, that may mean putting paint on a canvas or it may mean putting a pot on the stove. It may mean creating space for high schoolers to be honest about their mental health or creating an organization that supports single moms and lets them know they're not alone. It may mean waking up each morning and resolving to cultivate a household for your children saturated in love and kindness. All this is creative faithfulness to the story. The renowned painter Makoto Fujimura writes, "When we make, we invite the abundance of God's world into the reality of scarcity all about us."[14]

I'm Here from the Future

Every week at the Anglican church I attend, we recite the Nicene Creed, a statement of faith penned by a council of church fathers in the fourth century. Through a series of "We believe . . ." statements, together as a church we profess the core elements of our faith pertaining to God the Father, God the Son, and God the Holy Spirit. The creed comes to a close with this line: "We look for the resurrection of the dead, and the life of the world to come. Amen."

As Christians living in the already-but-not-yet of God's kingdom, we immerse ourselves in Scripture to know the story that has preceded us. But we also immerse ourselves in Scripture so we can anticipate the story still to come. Bartholomew and Goheen say that we are *pushed* forward by the story that has come before, by the impetus of Jesus' words and actions, and also *pulled* forward by our hope and expectation for his kingdom coming in its fullness.[15] Our eschatology (the set of beliefs we hold about our ultimate destiny) informs our actions in the present. "Ethics is lived eschatology," says J. Richard Middleton. Quoting New Testament scholar George Eldon Ladd, he calls it "the presence of the future."[16]

This is where the metaphor of the unfinished Shakespeare play breaks down a bit, because the Bible does give us hints and clues pointing toward the final act of the drama. We don't have to improvise the ending of the story; our calling as Christ followers is to faithfully bridge the gap and wait for the Lord to act. I've never had to build a bridge before, but I imagine it's important to have a clear sense both of where the bridge originates and also where it's supposed to arrive on the other side. That's why a biblical understanding of Act 6, the final act of the story, is so vital.

For so many people, the ultimate goal of the Christian life is to "go to heaven when I die." That's how the story ends. And while there's something to be said for our spirits being with Christ after our death, I'll reiterate that our ultimate hope is *resurrection*: for Death itself to be undone once and for all, for sin to be extinguished, for heaven and earth to be remade and reunited into a new creation, for God to come back to this place that he declared good and dwell with his children once again.

When Jesus walked out of that tomb early on Easter morning, he launched a new world right in the middle of the old one. He was, in the flesh, the presence of this hoped-for future. But it didn't stop there. John's Gospel describes a key sequence where Jesus appears to his disciples after the Resurrection, showing them the scars in his hands and his side. "Peace be with you," he says. "As the Father has sent me, so I am sending you." He breathes on them. "Receive the Holy Spirit."[17]

The Spirit is God's down payment on the future. Hebrews says that those who have partaken in the Holy Spirit have "tasted the good word of God and the powers of the age to come."[18] The full presence of the Father, Son, and Spirit will one day permeate all reality, yet baptism opens the door for that future to colonize our lives in the present.

As the Father sent the Son, so the Son sends us—into the world as signposts pointing toward this new creation future, showing and telling the world through word and deed that the future is already breaking in. Animated by the power of the Spirit, we faithfully improvise the story in our time not with the goal of evacuating souls to heaven but of allowing God to work through us as he brings his kingdom on earth as it is in heaven.

This is what it looks like to rediscover the human vocation given to us at the beginning of the biblical narrative: to create with God, to steward the earth on his behalf and participate in his work to bring flourishing upon it. The days we spend with the sun on our faces and the grass under our feet mean something. Our daily labor is not in vain. The Spirit can enchant even the most mundane parts of life because God will, somehow, assimilate them into something eternal.

"God invites us to co-create, but that does not mean that we are the ones to create the New Creation; only God can do that work," writes Fujimura.[19] But, nonetheless, "God is not just restoring us to Eden; God is creating through us a garden, an abundant city of God's Kingdom. What we build, design, and depict on this side of eternity matters, because in some mysterious way, those creations will become part of the future city of God."[20]

Of course, we improvise lives that point toward the new creation while remaining fully aware that we are still enmeshed in the darkness of the present evil age. Death surrounds us; evil lurks around every corner; violence rules the world's imagination; lies define the world's reality. Our hearts themselves are a battlefield between light and darkness. As such, the cocreating we do for the kingdom oftentimes must take place through our tears and our pain. The Spirit renovates our hearts while we go out to meet the world in its places of brokenness with a message of love, a message delivered through our own Cross-shaped lives.

Just as the icon of our faith is Christ on the cross, God's power in this in-between time looks remarkably like weakness. He restores through our brokenness. He heals through our wounds. "The victory of the cross will be implemented through the means of the cross," says Wright.[21]

Again, we follow the story that Scripture tells. Jesus received the Spirit upon his baptism and then proceeded to a life of weeping, rejection, abandonment, suffering, and death. Likewise, the apostles received the Spirit, and many of them went to their deaths. Paul writes repeatedly in his letters about the suffering he has endured for the sake of the gospel, often boasting about his weakness and celebrating his hardships. In his letter to the Romans, he says:

> If we're children, we are also heirs: heirs of God, and fellow heirs with the Messiah, as long as we suffer with him so that we may also be glorified with him.
>
> This is how I work it out. The sufferings we go through in the present time are not worth putting in the scale alongside the glory that is going to be unveiled for us. Yes: creation itself is on tiptoe with expectation, eagerly awaiting the moment when God's children will be revealed. . . .
>
> We know that the entire creation is groaning together, and going through labour pains together, up until the present time. Not only so: we too, we who have the

first fruits of the spirit's life within us, are groaning
within ourselves, as we eagerly await our adoption, the
redemption of our body.[22]

When we live into the Bible's story, centered on Christ, we see
that the story comes full circle—that God's intentions to live on
earth with his image bearers will not be thwarted, that sin and evil
and death will not have the final say. All creation is groaning for
this vision to be realized. The trees and rocks, lions and whales,
sun and stars are craning their necks, looking for Christ coming
on the clouds to meet his bride.

The Bible's story doesn't conclude with the End but with the
New. Just as Jesus' new body bore old scars, we can be assured that
as we pursue justice, peace, righteousness, truth, and beauty, our
accomplishments and our wounds will all be incorporated into the
everlasting kingdom. Somehow, mysteriously, the power of sacrificial love prepares the way for the consummation of the biblical
story and the beginning of something gloriously new.

As the Father sent Jesus, so he sends us—into the world as
people of hope, reaching out with signs of love in the midst of its
pain, always with our eyes on the horizon. Looking for the resurrection of the dead and the life of the world to come.

Epilogue

A COUPLE OF YEARS AGO, my family and I moved to a house in a more rural part of town. In the wintertime, the primary way we keep our home warm is with a big, black wood-burning stove in our living room.

Since I began tending the stove every day, I've learned a lot about the way oxygen influences fire—something I didn't have to consider as much with the outdoor campfires I've built. By manipulating the stove door and a couple of vents, I can regulate the amount of oxygen flowing into the fire and up the chimney. Lots of air will get the fire burning hot and bright, but it'll also make the wood burn up more quickly. So the trick is to give the fire plenty of oxygen as it gets going and then close off the various vents and reduce the airflow to a trickle for a long, slow burn.

Sometimes the fire will go unattended for several hours as we go about our day until, sometime in the midafternoon, I'll walk past the stove and notice the lack of heat. I'll crouch down and peer through the glass door only to see a pile of gray ash mixed with a few black chunks of former logs. *Shoot,* I'll think to myself. *We let it go out.*

But when I open the stove door, I hear the soft *whoosh* of oxygen rushing into the void, and I'm greeted by a pleasant surprise. The gray mass is suddenly bespeckled with little bits of glowing orange. I stir the coals around a bit, turn them over, and see that their underbellies are twinkling with warmth and color. I listen and notice that these remnants are crackling, ever so softly, with heat and energy and potential. All I had to do was disrupt the status quo.

If you've struggled to connect with the Bible, maybe it isn't your fault. Maybe you've inherited a set of flawed assumptions about what it means to read the Bible well. Maybe the "normal way" of using it is actually rife with barriers that prevent you from truly becoming immersed in its transformative story. Maybe all you needed was a disruptive invitation into something different, something new. Some fresh air to reignite those dormant embers.

My prayer is that this book has been a welcome disruption to a system that isn't working for you. Over the course of our journey together, we've covered quite a broad spectrum of changes you can incorporate to make a real difference in how you engage with Scripture. We explored the numerous ways the modern Bible obstructs the text and discourages reading and then proposed a new physical format that honors the Bible's literature and gives the sacred words room to breathe. We scrutinized some of the reading habits that have pervaded our Bible culture and then recovered the essential practices of reading big, reading in community, and reading in context. Finally, we reframed our fundamental understanding of what the Bible *is* and how it invites us to participate in the mission of God. It has certainly been a lot to process, but time and time again I've seen how the changes you've read about make Scripture come alive for people in ways they never thought possible. They did for me. I hope they do for you.

Now, I've read books like this before too. Books that suggest so much sweeping change that by the end I feel paralyzed because I'm not sure where to even begin. If you feel this way, here's my advice: Start by getting a reader's Bible. I mentioned the version our team created in chapter 3, but there are other options (with various features and layouts, so do some research) available in a number of translations.

Using a Bible that isn't governed by chapters and verses is the best place to start on this journey. It'll allow your brain to relax and just read, clearing the path for you to get absorbed in the flow of the stories, songs, and letters. Read with no agenda. Read to enjoy. See what God does.

From there, the next best step is to invite others into the experience. See if some friends or family members want to read, and then gather together for a conversation. Less like a Bible study, more like a book club. The Bible operates best when it's in the center of a community that is feasting on its books and discussing them together. Over time, you'll begin to see how these books connect into a story and, as we've explored, how you and your community are invited to step in and live the drama.

However you decide to begin making these changes, I urge you:

Make changes. You didn't pick up a book called *The Bible Reset* because you were satisfied with how things were going between you and the Bible. And yet it's easy to get swept back up in the current of *regular* Bibles and *regular* devotionals because that's what everyone else is doing. It's the only thing they know.

"Nothing changes at the center," says writer Russell Banks. "Change only occurs at the edges and works its way in."[1] Change happens when we have our assumptions stripped away so we can begin to reconsider norms and ideas we've always taken for granted. It happens at the end of our comfort zones, when we're willing to step away from that familiar thing that isn't actually working for us. It happens when we're brave enough to swim against the current, push back against the status quo, and fight for something better.

There's a growing group of us around the edges who are doing things differently with the Bible. We believe things don't have to stay the way they are just because that's how they've been. We see a new way forward, a fresh invitation that is truer and more authentic to the Bible God gave us, that opens up this strange and sacred gift to be experienced in all its fullness.

Will you join us?

Acknowledgments

WHEN I BEGAN WRITING THIS BOOK, I also started reading the acknowledgments pages of every book I finished, looking forward to the day when I'd get the chance to write my own. This book has truly been a group effort, and I'm deeply grateful to everyone who has made it possible for you to be holding it in your hands.

To my brothers at the Institute for Bible Reading: Glenn Paauw, Scott Bolinder, Paul Caminiti, and Jim Steere, thank you for teaching me and showing me what it means to read and live the Bible well. I've learned more from you all than you'll ever know. To John Sloan, literary genius and editing giant, thank you for sending me on my way and assuring me that I have the right stuff to write this book. That meant the world coming from you.

Thank you to Bob Fryling for sharing my work with the NavPress team. Thank you to Dave Zimmerman, Deborah Sáenz Gonzalez, and the rest of the good folks at NavPress for taking a chance on an unknown, first-time author. Your courage is rare these days. Thank you for helping me craft this book and make it better.

To my beautiful wife, Lacey, you're the only one this book could ever be dedicated to. Thank you for your willingness to read my rough drafts and to help me think through many half-baked ideas, whether scribbled on a whiteboard or rambled out across the dinner table. Thank you for your steadfast encouragement and warm smile. To my two little ones, Jack and Ellie, thank you for bursting into my office with many sacred interruptions over the years—timely reminders that I'm deeply loved no matter how the writing is going. I hope this book means something to you one day.

Mom and Dad, thank you for bringing the three of us to church every week, and for dragging us there when we begged you not to make us go. Thank you for always cheering me on.

Finally, to Rachel Dewey, thank you for giving me that strange edition of the Bible without any numbers in it. Without you I never would have begun this journey. Until we meet again, rest in peace.

Notes

CHAPTER 1 | WE CAN DO BETTER

1. Jordan Golson, "We can't tell if Elon Musk is joking about his next 'boring' company," The Verge, December 17, 2016, https://www.theverge .com/2016/12/17/13993754/elon-musk-tunnel-boring-tesla-spacex. This introductory story about Musk was based on the series of tweets cited in this article, with added narrative embellishments by the author. The phrase "soul-destroying traffic" was taken from The Boring Company website: https://www.boringcompany.com, accessed January 20, 2023.
2. Acts 21:18, ESV.
3. C. S. Lewis, *Mere Christianity* (1952; repr. ed., New York: HarperCollins, 2001), 28.

CHAPTER 2 | SIX FEET UNDER

1. Christopher R. Smith, *After Chapters and Verses* (Colorado Springs: Biblica Publishing, 2010), 17.
2. Pitts Theology Library, *The Printer's Device: Robert Estienne's Numbering of Verses and the Changing Form of the New Testament in the 15th and 16th Centuries,* trans. Armin Siedlecki (Pitts Theology Library Digital Image Archive, 2013), 29.
3. Smith, *After Chapters,* 8.
4. Joni Mitchell, "Big Yellow Taxi," *Ladies of the Canyon* © 1970 Reprise Records.
5. Nicholas Carr, *The Shallows: What the Internet Is Doing to Our Brains* (New York: W. W. Norton & Company, 2011), 44.
6. Carr, *The Shallows,* 45.
7. Jacques Le Goff, *Time, Work, and Culture in the Middle Ages,* trans. Arthur Goldhammer (Chicago: University of Chicago Press, 1982), 44.
8. Mary Oliver, *Upstream: Selected Essays* (New York: Penguin Press, 2016), 25.

9. Oliver, *Upstream*, 25.

10. Smith, *After Chapters*, 34.

11. This image was created by Julie Nor-Barber of Flair Studio (flairstudio.net) for the Institute of Bible Reading and is included here with permission.

12. Maryanne Wolf, *Reader, Come Home: The Reading Brain in a Digital World* (New York: HarperCollins Publishers, 2018), 71.

13. Wolf, *Reader, Come Home*, 72.

14. Carr, *The Shallows*, 7.

15. Patricia M. Greenfield, "Technology and Informal Education: What Is Taught, What Is Learned," *Science* 323, no. 5910 (Jan. 2, 2009): 71.

16. Andy Crouch, *Culture Making: Recovering Our Creative Calling* (Downers Grove, IL: InterVarsity Press, 2008), 23.

CHAPTER 3 | DIGGING UP THE REAL BIBLE

1. Karen Wolman (quoting Fabrizio Mancinelli), "Washing away grime or an artist's genius? A shade of doubt dogs the Sistine Chapel restoration," *The Christian Science Monitor*, September 11, 1986, https://www.csmonitor. com/1986/0911/lsist-f.html.

2. Karen Swallow Prior, *On Reading Well: Finding the Good Life through Great Books* (Grand Rapids, MI: Brazos Press, 2018), 16.

3. Prior, *On Reading Well*, 16.

4. Walter Isaacson, "How Steve Jobs' Love of Simplicity Fueled a Design Revolution," *Smithsonian Magazine*, September 2012, https://www .smithsonianmag.com/arts-culture/how-steve-jobs-love-of-simplicity -fueled-a-design-revolution-23868877.

5. Christopher R. Smith, *After Chapters and Verses* (Colorado Springs: Biblica Publishing, 2010), 90.

6. "How to Make a Reader's Bible w/ Christopher Smith," interview by Alex Goodwin, Glenn Paauw, and Paul Caminiti, *The Bible Reset*, October 7, 2020, podcast, 49:42, https://instituteforbiblereading.org/episode-5-how -to-make-a-readers-bible-christopher-smith.

7. Revelation 21:1.

8. "Immerse at Bethesda Community Church," YouTube video, 6:03, July 10, 2019, https://youtu.be/Qo6R-mFjFZs.

9. "Southern Wesleyan University Students' Lives 'Rocked' Reading Immerse," YouTube video, 5:16, July 9, 2019, https://youtu.be/H1QahGUzdf8.

10. Farcroft Group, "Triumph or Travesty? The Controversial Restoration of the Sistine Chapel," February 21, 2020, https://www.farcroftgroup.com/the -controversial-restoration-of-the-sistine-chapel. For more on this, see http:// www.robertfulford.com/restore.html. The restoration is admittedly the subject

of some controversy in the art community, with critics claiming that the restorers stripped away too many layers and inadvertently removed some of the shadow and definition that Michelangelo had originally incorporated into the frescoes. The restorers stand by their methods. "We are now probably seeing what people saw for the first fifty years after Michelangelo painted," said the lead restorer (https://www.csmonitor.com/1986/0911/lsist-f.html).

CHAPTER 4 | READ BIG

1. Maryanne Wolf, *Reader, Come Home: The Reading Brain in a Digital World* (New York: HarperCollins Publishers, 2018), 75.
2. Craig G. Bartholomew and Michael W. Goheen, *The Drama of Scripture: Finding Our Place in the Biblical Story* (Grand Rapids, MI: Baker Academic, 2004), 12.
3. Philip Yancey, in a conversation with the author.
4. Eugene Peterson, *Eat This Book: A Conversation in the Art of Spiritual Reading* (Grand Rapids, MI: Wm. B. Eerdmans Publishing Co., 2006), 59.
5. As quoted in John Ortberg, "Ruthlessly Eliminate Hurry," *Christianity Today*, July 4, 2002, https://www.christianitytoday.com/pastors/2002/july-online-only/cln20704.html.
6. Karl Barth, *The Word of God & The Word of Man*, trans. Douglas Horton (1928; repr. ed., Gloucester, MA: Peter Smith, 1978), 23.
7. Barth, *Word of God*, 24.
8. Barth, *Word of God*, 24.
9. Isaiah 43:19. (Yes, the publisher asked that I at least include chapter-and-verse references in the notes.)
10. Barth, *Word of God*, 27.
11. Barth, *Word of God*, 28.
12. Barth, *Word of God*, 29.
13. Barth, *Word of God*, 25.

CHAPTER 5 | READ TOGETHER

1. Luke 2:46-47, NTFE.
2. Luke 2:48, MSG.
3. Luke 2:49, NTFE.
4. Nehemiah 7:73–8:1, NLT.
5. Jordan J. Ryan, *The Role of the Synagogue in the Aims of Jesus* (Minneapolis, MN: Fortress Press, 2017), 69.
6. Luke 4:15, NLT.
7. Luke 4:16, NLT, emphasis added.
8. Acts 17:2-3.

9. 1 Timothy 4:13.

10. Justin Martyr, "The First Apology of Justin Martyr," Chapter 67, *Ante-Nicene Fathers*, Vol. 1, ed. Alexander Roberts, James Donaldson, and A. Cleveland Coxe; trans. Marcus Dods and George Reith (Buffalo, NY: Christian Literature Publishing Co., 1885.), rev. and ed. Kevin Knight, New Advent, https://www.newadvent.org/fathers/0126.htm.

11. Dr. Seuss, *Oh, the Places You'll Go!* (New York: Random House, 1990), 2.

12. Scot McKnight, *A Community Called Atonement* (Nashville, TN: Abingdon Press, 2007), 119.

13. McKnight, *Community Called Atonement*, 145.

14. Quoted in Glenn R. Paauw, *Saving the Bible from Ourselves: Learning to Read and Live the Bible Well* (Downers Grove, IL: InterVarsity Press, 2016), 169.

15. Esau McCaulley, *Reading While Black: African American Biblical Interpretation as an Exercise in Hope* (Downers Grove, IL: InterVarsity Press, 2020), 91.

16. Ephesians 3:17-18, emphasis added.

17. Ephesians 6:13-17, NLT.

CHAPTER 6 | DISCOVER THE BIBLE'S WORLD

1. "Comedy Central Presents: Brian Regan," season 3, episode 14, September 7, 2000. https://www.cc.com/episodes/6cqjhh/comedy-central-presents-brian-regan-season-3-ep-14.

2. Ben Witherington III, *Reading and Understanding the Bible* (New York: Oxford University Press, 2014), 96.

3. E. Randolph Richards and Richard James, *Misreading Scripture with Individualist Eyes: Patronage, Honor, and Shame in the Biblical World* (Downers Grove, IL: InterVarsity Press, 2020), 2.

4. Quoted in Dan Kimball, *How (Not) to Read the Bible: Making Sense of the Anti-women, Anti-science, Pro-violence, Pro-slavery, and Other Crazy-Sounding Parts of Scripture* (Grand Rapids, MI: Zondervan Publishers, 2020), 121.

5. Kimball, *How (Not) to Read the Bible*, 120–21. Kimball cites *Menahot* 43b for this prayer.

6. Although my editors and I ultimately decided to use the term *Old Testament* rather than *First Testament* throughout this book, I believe it's important to resist the connotation associated with *Old* as unnecessary or irrelevant. Deep familiarity with the Old Testament will help us better understand the life and ministry of Jesus as he fulfilled the old covenant and instituted the new.

7. Kimball, *How (Not) to Read the Bible*, 121.

8. Carolyn Custis James, "Dismantling Patriarchy and Recovering the Blessed Alliance," *Carolyn Custis James* (blog), March 25, 2021, https://carolyncustis james.com/2021/03/25/dismantling-patriarchy-and-recovering-the-blessed -alliance.

9. Richards and James, *Misreading Scripture*, 19.

10. Matthew 12:48-50.

11. "How the Bible Helps Us Talk about Racism - Dominique Gilliard, Michelle Sanchez, Fr. Steve Delaney," YouTube video, 1:01:15, June 26, 2020, https:// instituteforbiblereading.org/how-bibles-story-helps-us-talk-about-racism.

12. 1 Corinthians 1:4, NLT.

13. Philippians 1:3, NLT.

14. Galatians 1:6, NLT.

15. Revelation 17:9, NLT.

16. "How to Read the Bible: Apocalyptic Literature," YouTube video, 6:57, June 9, 2020, https://youtu.be/UNDX4tUdj1Y.

17. Proverbs 1:22-23.

18. Proverbs 22:6, ESV.

19. Ecclesiastes 1:2.

20. Ecclesiastes 12:13.

21. Job 40:2, NLT.

22. Job 42:6, NLT.

23. Kenneth E. Bailey, *Jesus through Middle Eastern Eyes: Cultural Studies in the Gospels* (Downers Grove, IL: InterVarsity Press, 2008), 281.

CHAPTER 7 | THE STORY WE FIND OURSELVES IN

1. Dictionary.com, s.v. "paradigm (*n.*)," accessed January 17, 2023, https:// www.dictionary.com/browse/paradigm.

2. Eugene Peterson, *Eat This Book: A Conversation in the Art of Spiritual Reading* (Grand Rapids, MI: Wm. B. Eerdmans Publishing Co., 2006), 40.

3. Antonio Damasio, *The Feeling of What Happens: Body and Emotion in the Making of Consciousness* (New York: Harcourt Brace, 1999), 30, quoted in Dan P. McAdams, Ruthellen Josselson, and Amia Lieblich, eds. *Identity and Story: Creating Self in Narrative* (Washington, DC: American Psychological Association, 2006), introduction.

4. See McAdams, Josselson, and Lieblich, *Identity and Story*, introduction.

5. Alasdair MacIntyre, *After Virtue: A Study in Moral Theory*, 2nd ed. (Notre Dame, IN: University of Notre Dame Press, 1984), 216, quoted in James K. A. Smith, *You Are What You Love: The Spiritual Power of Habit* (Grand Rapids, MI: Brazos Press, 2016), 89.

6. Genesis 1:1, ESV.

7. John 19:30.

8. Stuart Murray, *The Naked Anabaptist: The Bare Essentials of a Radical Faith* (Independence, MO: Herald Press, 2015), 69.

9. Luke 1:16-17.

10. Dennis R. Edwards, *What Is the Bible and How Do We Understand It?* (Independence, MO: Herald Press, 2019), 45.

11. N. T. Wright, *Surprised by Scripture: Engaging Contemporary Issues* (San Francisco: HarperOne, 2014), 28.

12. Matthew 5:17.

13. Luke 24:21.

14. Luke 24:25-27.

15. Peter Enns, *Inspiration and Incarnation: Evangelicals and the Problem of the Old Testament*, 2nd ed. (Grand Rapids, MI: Baker Academic, 2015), 152.

16. Michael F. Bird, *Seven Things I Wish Christians Knew about the Bible* (Grand Rapids, MI: Zondervan, 2021), 183.

17. Scot McKnight, *A Community Called Atonement* (Nashville, TN: Abingdon Press, 2007), 145.

18. N. T. Wright and Michael F. Bird, *The New Testament in Its World: An Introduction to the History, Literature, and Theology of the First Christians* (Grand Rapids, MI: Zondervan Academic, 2019), 881–82.

19. Wright and Bird, *The New Testament in Its World*, 881.

20. James K. A. Smith, *You Are What You Love: The Spiritual Power of Habit* (Grand Rapids, MI: Brazos Press, 2016), 45–46.

21. Walter Brueggemann, *A Way Other Than Our Own: Devotions for Lent* (Louisville, KY: Westminster John Knox Press, 2017), 3.

22. Of course, this critique isn't meant to absolve the younger generations of our responsibility. We have certainly chosen our own paths and allowed ourselves to get caught up in a myriad of alternative stories. My point is that there is a lot of room for improvement in how self-identified followers of Jesus tell and demonstrate the narrative of Scripture and the Good News of Christ.

23. Lesslie Newbigin, *Foolishness to the Greeks: The Gospel and Western Culture* (Grand Rapids, MI: Eerdmans, 1986), 61.

24. Smith has a great chapter on this topic in *You Are What You Love*: "What Story Are You In? The Narrative Arc of Formative Christian Worship."

25. McKnight, *Community Called Atonement*, 146.

26. Wright and Bird, *The New Testament in Its World*, 881.

CHAPTER 8 | THE SIX-ACT DRAMA OF SCRIPTURE

1. Genesis 1:1-2.

2. Genesis 1:3.

3. John H. Walton, *The Lost World of Genesis One: Ancient Cosmology and the Origins Debate* (Downers Grove, IL: InterVarsity Press, 2009), 59.

4. Walton, *Lost World of Genesis One*, 71.
5. Walton, *Lost World of Genesis One*, 72.
6. Scot McKnight, *A Community Called Atonement* (Nashville, TN: Abingdon Press, 2007), 21.
7. Genesis 2:16-17.
8. Christopher Nolan, dir., *Inception* (Burbank, CA: Warner Bros, 2010).
9. Genesis 3:4-5.
10. Craig G. Bartholomew and Michael W. Goheen, *The Drama of Scripture: Finding Our Place in the Biblical Story* (Grand Rapids, MI: Baker Academic, 2004), 43.
11. Genesis 6:5.
12. Genesis 9:11, 15.
13. Genesis 10:22-23, NLT.
14. Genesis 12:2-3, emphasis added.
15. Gordon J. Wenham, *Story as Torah: Reading the Old Testament Narrative Ethically* (Edinburgh: T & T Clark, 2000), 37.
16. Exodus 19:4-6.
17. Luke 1:30-33.
18. Bartholomew and Goheen, *Drama of Scripture*, 133.
19. Mark 1:11.
20. Mark 10:33-34.
21. N. T. Wright, *The Day the Revolution Began: Reconsidering the Meaning of Jesus's Crucifixion* (San Francisco, CA: HarperOne, 2016), 170.
22. Wright, *The Day the Revolution Began*, 179.
23. Luke 24:5-6.
24. Matthew 28:18-20.
25. Bartholomew and Goheen, *Drama of Scripture*, 168–69.
26. Matthew 28:20.
27. Acts 1:3, NLT.
28. Acts 2:32-33, 36.
29. Bartholomew and Goheen, *Drama of Scripture*, 172.
30. Matthew 6:10.
31. Matthew 19:28.
32. Acts 3:21, NLT.
33. John 19:30.
34. Colossians 1:15-20, emphasis added.
35. Revelation 21:1-5.
36. N. T. Wright and Michael F. Bird, *The New Testament in Its World: An Introduction to the History, Literature, and Theology of the First Christians* (Grand Rapids, MI: Zondervan Academic, 2019), 889.

CHAPTER 9 | NEW CREATION IMPROV

1. J. R. R. Tolkien, *The Return of the King: Being the Third Part of The Lord of the Rings* (1955; repr. ed., London: HarperCollins Publishers, 2004), 1016.
2. Tolkien, *Return of the King*, 1020.
3. N. T. Wright, *Scripture and the Authority of God: How to Read the Bible Today* (San Francisco, CA: HarperOne, 2011), 127.
4. Samuel Wells, *Improvisation: The Drama of Christian Ethics* (Grand Rapids, MI: Brazos Press, 2004), 57.
5. Eugene Peterson, *A Long Obedience in the Same Direction* (Downer's Grove, IL: InterVarsity Press, 1980).
6. As quoted in Geoffrey C. Ward and Ken Burns, *Jazz: A History of America's Music* (New York: Alfred A. Knopf, 2000), 375.
7. Micah 6:8.
8. Mark 12:30, NLT; see also Deuteronomy 6:5.
9. Mark 12:31; Leviticus 19:18, NLT.
10. Isaiah 2:4.
11. Rosaria Butterfield, *The Gospel Comes with a House Key* (Wheaton, IL: Crossway, 2018).
12. CityGate Network (https://www.citygatenetwork.org/agrm/About.asp) supports over three hundred faith-based crisis shelters and life-transformation centers across North America.
13. Dorothy L. Sayers, *The Mind of the Maker* (San Francisco: HarperCollins, 1968), 22.
14. Makoto Fujimura, *Art and Faith: A Theology of Making* (New Haven, CT: Yale University Press, 2021), 4.
15. Craig G. Bartholomew and Michael W. Goheen, *The Drama of Scripture: Finding Our Place in the Biblical Story* (Grand Rapids, MI: Baker Academic, 2004), 206.
16. J. Richard Middleton, *A New Heaven and a New Earth: Reclaiming Biblical Eschatology* (Grand Rapids, MI: Baker Academic, 2014), 24.
17. John 20:21-22, NLT.
18. Hebrews 6:5, NASB.
19. Fujimura, *Art and Faith*, 35.
20. Fujimura, *Art and Faith*, 12.
21. N. T. Wright, *The Day the Revolution Began: Reconsidering the Meaning of Jesus's Crucifixion* (San Francisco, CA: HarperOne, 2016), 366.
22. Romans 8:17-19, 22-23, NTfE.

EPILOGUE

1. Russell Banks, *Mark Twain*, directed by Ken Burns, episode 2, aired January 14, 2002, on PBS, https://www.pbs.org/kenburns/mark-twain.

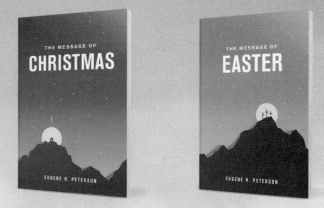
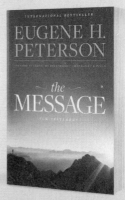

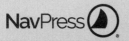

EASILY READ AND UNDERSTAND THE BOOKS OF LUKE AND ACTS.

Immerse: Luke & Acts allows you to read this portion of the Bible on your own or enjoy and discuss it with friends and groups.

Immerse takes you on a unique journey through the Bible as it was originally created—without chapter or verse breaks. Created with the look and feel of a paperback book and in the clear and trusted New Living Translation, *Immerse* enables you to easily read and understand the Bible.

+ + +

IMMERSE YOURSELF IN THE ENTIRE BIBLE!

ImmerseBible.com